CROSSING
A True Story

Glyn Vincent

City Point Press

Copyright © 2025 by Glyn Vincent
Hardcover ISBN 978-1-947951-81-5
eBook ISBN 978-1-947951-82-2

All rights reserved.
No portion of this book may be reproduced in any fashion, print, facsimile, or electronic means, or by any method yet to be developed, without the express written permission of the publisher. This is a work of nonfiction. Some names and identifying details of people have been changed.

Book and cover design by Barbara Aronica
Cover photograph by Glyn Vincent

Chapter 2, "Limbas," is adapted, in part, from a story, "Hotel Bolivar," first published in *Mr. Beller's Neighborhood: New York Stories*.

Grateful acknowledgment is given for permission to use W. S. Merwin, "Odysseus," from *The First Four Books of Poems*. Copyright © 1960, 2000 by W. S. Merwin. Reprinted with the permission of The Permissions Company, LLC, on behalf of Copper Canyon Press, coppercanyonpress.org.

Excerpt from *Kafka on the Shore* by Haruki Murakami, translated by Philip Gabriel, translation copyright © 2005 by Haruki Murakami Archival Labyrinth. Used by permission of Alfred A. Knopf, an imprint of the Knopf Doubleday Publishing Group, a division of Penguin Random House LLC. All rights reserved.

Manufactured in the United States of America

Published by
City Point Press
PO Box 2063
Westport, CT 06880
www.citypointpress.com
Distributed by Simon and Schuster
www.simonandschuster.biz

To Stacy

CONTENTS

PROLOGUE: Nowhere   ix

PART I
Doubt

1 | Happy Bay   3

2 | *Limbas*   11

3 | The Captain   26

4 | Leaving the World Behind   41

5 | A Sleeping Whale   49

6 | Hallucinations and a Shit Show   62

7 | Absence   75

8 | Containment   90

9 | Release   95

10 | Days and Nights   99

11 | Stuffed Animals and the Sea   109

12 | Five Hundred Miles   115

13 | Cotopaxi   121

14 | Spinnakers, Risotto, and Latitude   126

15 | Faraway Shores   131

PART II
The Storm

16 | The Weather Map	137
17 | Good Winds and Bad	141
18 | Passages	148
19 | Gales and a Long-Beaked Bird	160
20 | The Eye of the Storm	165
21 | Something Happened	169
22 | Multiple Lives	172
23 | Sincerity	183
24 | Sixty-knot Winds	188
25 | Losing Control	193
26 | Almost There	199
27 | Midnight	203
28 | Destinations	207
EPILOGUE: Somewhere	213
ACKNOWLEDGMENTS	219

Sometimes fate is like a small sandstorm that keeps changing directions. You change direction but the sandstorm chases you. You turn again, but the storm adjusts. Over and over you play this out. . . . Why? Because this storm isn't something that blew in from far away, something that has nothing to do with you. This storm is you. Something inside of you. So all you can do is give in to it, step right inside the storm . . . and walk through it step by step.

—Haruki Murakami, *Kafka on the Shore*

PROLOGUE: NOWHERE

Wednesday, April 13
N 34.21, W 42.57

Yesterday is a blur. The seas were high, the sky bright as the day started. But it did not last long. Soon we were being buffeted by squalls with the approach of another low. The wind came up relentlessly to gale force, making the shrouds moan, an eerie sound that seemed to comment on the folly of our journey. Not just ours but those that had crossed the same ocean before us, the history of hope and misery, the journeys toward freedom and slavery. The ships that never made it through. The passengers whose last breaths were of icy seawater.

At dusk, the captain left me alone at the helm. Yves and Nikos had gone below to sleep a few hours before. I wondered why it was taking them so long to show up or turn on the lights. My hands were cramping on the wheel, my arms and shoulders felt like lead. The companionway was closed because of the waves breaking on deck and intermittent downpours. I was cut off from the rest of the crew. One mistake and I could be swept into the sea without anyone knowing. My thoughts closed in again about the captain, his erratic moods and intentions. Was it all in my head? I'd had so many bad feelings and premonitions on the way to taking this trip. Were they about to come true?

• • •

A few weeks earlier, on a blustery March morning, I was looking out the airplane window as we inched away from New York and the East Coast shoreline. The dark Atlantic ten thousand feet below us was speckled indiscriminately with white dots, wave spit, rolls of foam that unraveled as the bitter cold wind whipped up the sea. I glanced up at the clouds floating in the serene sky, but my gaze was pulled back down. I spotted two container ships, immobile, waiting offshore for their turn to enter port. Then, for the next three and a half hours and seventeen hundred miles, there was no evidence of man on the surface of the sea.

Scrunched in my airline seat, I was engulfed by a wave of dread and regret. Why wasn't I just going for a stress-free Caribbean vacation with my wife, Stacy, who was reading next to me, and our two close friends, Yves and Pamela, seated behind us on the plane? Snorkeling in the clear, warm water, Caribbean seafood dinners, a hike or two, some reading, and then back to our lives in New York.

Instead, I was about to embark on a sailboat with Yves and a captain and crew we didn't know to cross the Atlantic from St. Martin to the Azores in Portugal at a time of year when the ocean was still raked with late-winter gales. Casualties occur every year. It's not a journey to be attempted without experience and preparation. I had a few basic sailing certificates, but I was a middle-aged amateur sailor who had never been out of sight of land, more inherently cautious than a risk-taker. What was I trying to prove? Why did I want to sail across the Atlantic?

I looked out the window beyond the puffy clouds to the meeting point of sea and sky. The horizon called out to me, as it has since I was a boy with my nose pressed up against the cold Plexiglas window of a plane. What was this hard-to-define ache to be drawn out into the waves whose colors change every hour?

My infatuation with the sea goes way back, but I had few childhood nautical experiences. No one in my immediate family was a sailor or had anything to do with marine life other than occasionally visiting the seashore in summer. Or so I once thought. It turned out there *was* an important link: an original voyage in 1869—across part of the Mediterranean from Syria to Egypt—that led to other sea crossings, further ruptures, and new departures.

Going to sea can be a way out of a predicament on land. Proverbially, misfits, fugitives, and the disinherited became sailors to get what had been denied them on shore, be it money, adventure, or social advancement. Some were drawn by what the American novelist Herman Melville called the "mystical vibration" of being out of sight of land, perhaps, beyond the call of duty or reproach. Romantically, the ocean has represented a form of reverie, an escape. Who has not stood on a lonely promontory, the end of a dock or beach and wondered what lies beyond the watery horizon, what future it might offer?

Throughout history, emigrants have approached the sea reluctantly to seek salvation from political and economic hardship. My parents spent their itinerant childhoods in Europe and the Middle East. My father was born in Algeria and raised, after the age of six, in France. My mother, the daughter of a German count, left Berlin for the United States with her mother (whose family roots were American) when she was four. They and the generation before them were buffeted by war and dislocation. Resilient, they crossed seas and oceans to start new lives.

My trip, I felt as I approached its beginning, had something to do with their own voyages and eventual arrival in America. Their journeys informed who they became and how they saw the world. In postwar New York, my parents, like many other young American arrivals, celebrated their survival and newfound identity. My mother and father did so with ambition and reckless abandon; after decades of itinerant life, they didn't know how to stand still and start a family. They lived a tabloid existence, ricocheting from one crisis to the next. My father, when present, was bewildering, a seemingly warmhearted and funny man shadowed by a legacy of unrealized identities, lies, delusion, and violence.

I suspected as our jet descended toward St. Martin that my decision to sail across the ocean had something to do with who he was or wasn't; it was a reckoning with the past and the person I'd chosen to become. To stand up, to get off the plane, I had to assemble a smile for my wife and friends. I had to fend off the panicky feeling that the cards had been dealt, my fate already determined. I had to convince myself I was *not* going to end up alone on the deck of a boat, stuck in the middle of a restless ocean with storm clouds closing in on all sides.

PART I
Doubt

CHAPTER 1

Happy Bay

By the time we dove into the warm, wavy Caribbean water in the cove, it was almost sunset.

Stacy and I were swimming with our friends. Yves, still wiry and athletic, set out at a fast crawl for a white buoy fifty yards offshore, and I followed behind him. It was Yves who had taken hold of my dream to sail across the Atlantic *one day* and turned it into reality.

"That's it! Here we are!" he said to me when I caught up at the buoy. He was exuberant and seemingly unconcerned about the dangers of the adventure we were about to embark on. We high-fived and swam back toward shore. On the beach, we joined our wives and dried ourselves. By then we were mostly speechless. Dizzy from age and travel fatigue, we slowly walked back up the dusty road, taking in the scent of poisonous oleander and dry earth.

We had rented a modern all-white two-bedroom "villa" with wide views of the bay. There were rows of identical condos—some recently finished, others still being constructed. During the day we heard the flat knock of distant hammers, their terraces being dug out of the sedimentary, ocher-green hillside. Off on the horizon, the gray outline of a volcanic peak rose from the sea like an illustration in a children's adventure book.

The first evening, after our swim, we ate outside in the small garden and discussed the next day's plans. I was anxious to meet the captain and see the boat that would carry Yves and me on a twenty-six-hundred-mile trip to the Azores off the Portuguese coast where I had decided to disembark and visit the islands. Yves's plan was to continue sailing to Spain where he would meet Pamela.

"It's strange he hasn't sent us information on when and where to meet," I said to Yves who had found the captain online.

"He's probably just busy getting the boat ready," Yves said.

"Still, you'd think he'd be in touch," Pamela said.

There was a silence at the table. No one wanted to push the matter, but our wives, too, were curious. In the end, we decided to visit the marina the next day, unannounced.

In the morning, after a swim and breakfast, I drove the rent-a-car with Yves and Pamela in the back seat, along the narrow coast road. The route was clogged with traffic. Stacy, seated in front beside me, flinched as young men on scooters dodged and weaved between the lines of shiny cars. A breeze pushed shadowy clouds above us.

"You remember when Glyn drove us back to Havana at night?" Yves said, referring to a trip to Cuba we had taken in the '90s.

"It was a good thing he was at the wheel," Pamela chuckled in her low, raspy voice. A sense of direction was a trait, Yves's wife never failed to point out, her husband was sorely missing.

At the marina we stepped onto the floating piers and saw

the boat, *Orion*, directly in front of us, tied up alongside the dock. It looked small and weather-beaten. An aging, low-slung sailboat easily swallowed by a rogue wave.

"Are you sure this is it?" Stacy asked.

"It doesn't look like fifty-two feet," I said, keeping my voice neutral.

"I'll check." Yves paced out the length of the boat. "It's sixteen meters!" he announced with a note of triumph.

The paint on the mast was peeling and worn away to the aluminum beneath. There were lines, clothes, a life ring, an outboard engine, and other items hanging or mounted to the rails. One of the foresails looked like it would soon need to be replaced. Two deck vents had been covered with duct tape.

"What's going on there?" Stacy asked me, pointing to an open locker in the cockpit with parts and greasy tools spread about.

"He's working on something."

The captain's and his girlfriend's bathing suits were drying on the cabin roof. Their leather sandals were separated—one pair on the deck, another left carelessly on the pier. We called out, but there was no response from below.

To kill time, we strolled along the piers looking at other, bigger, more impressive and well-tended boats and then, unable to find the captain, we got back in the car.

On the way farther up the coast, we were mostly silent.

"Looks like the boat needs some work," I ventured.

"He lives on the boat. You can be sure he knows every inch of it," Yves said.

"Let's hope he has the money to make the needed repairs."

Orion

Left unsaid was the fact that Yves and I would soon be more than a thousand miles away at sea on a tired-looking boat with a captain we still had not met. There was no recourse if something went wrong, and obviously no getting off. We would be beyond the reach of rescue helicopters or coast guard boats for most of the trip. In fact, even with today's technology, the middle of the ocean is still the most remote and isolated place you can be on earth.

We drove to a seaside town and found an empty, linen-tabled French restaurant on the water. The waiter seated us on the terrace overlooking the bay and we ordered lunch. Yves was excited and drank a rum punch and two glasses of Chablis. He was psyched we had found the boat. That it existed was almost tantamount to Yves, a perpetual optimist, to having reached the other side of the ocean. Cheered by the good food and picturesque surroundings, the rest of us fell in with his elated mood and, by the end of our lunch, had decided to go to a secluded sandy spit of beach the waiter told us about.

"It's called Happy Bay," the waiter said, pointing across the water between two hilltops. "Be careful. It's difficult to find."

On the way, I took a narrow street to the right, circumventing a trash barrel that had been placed in the middle of the road.

"I think I'm on a dead end," I said slowing the car.

"Go ahead!" Yves barked tipsily. "Let's see where it leads!"

I came to a gate and passed it too quickly. We had entered a narrow, walled cemetery; there was nowhere to turn around. We were surrounded by graves—rectangular, above-ground sarcophagi decorated with empty bottles of rum and plastic flowers. Pam and Yves were giggling, but my stomach sank. This was a *bad omen*. I had reached the end of the street, a patch of ground littered with garbage, old clothes, condoms, and, in front of us, a deep, green river.

I don't think of myself as superstitious, but the wrong turn into the cemetery triggered an apprehensiveness that went back to my childhood. When I was ten or eleven, as my parents were separating, I would sit at my grandmother's small round dining table where she would do tarot card readings for family, friends, and paying visitors. My father's mother was a small, harmless woman with curled white hair who liked to cook and laugh, but whose demeanor became serious as she carefully placed down the cards in rows on the table for a session of prophecy after Sunday lunch. It seemed to me that she was particularly concerned about *my* prospects.

My sister's future always appeared glowingly conventional—a good marriage or two, children, financial security. With me things were muddier, ambiguous. Inevitably she turned over the Death card—a caped skeleton swinging a sickle or riding a white horse. She'd deftly bury the card, explaining that it didn't necessarily mean literal death but also transformation and the start of something new. Still, it was the frightening image of the Grim Reaper that stayed with me.

A mile back down the main road we found another right turn, a narrow strip of broken concrete that led to a dilapidated, locked gate and guardhouse. There was a large "No Trespassing" sign, but cars were parked on the shoulder of the street and a footpath ran through a break in the wall.

"Let's go for it," Yves said.

We walked up a long, wide slope of dry grass. In the bushes we saw junked cars and a wrecked boat. At the top of the hill we faced a line of abandoned resort houses—their roofs, doors, and windows all missing, their insides gutted. The development had been left untended for years. There were placards on the airport walls about the island's effort to rebuild after a Category 5 storm hit in 2017 with winds approaching three hundred kilometers an hour. "It must've been destroyed by the hurricane," I said.

The ruined resort reminded me of recent alarming news. A week before we left for St. Martin, the Azorean island of São Jorge was struck by thousands of mini earthquakes in a single day. The tremors continued for more than a week. Seismologists were bracing for a major volcanic eruption; thousands of people were being evacuated. A wary friend, who was a professor of statistics, warned me about the possibility of tsunamis. I imagined arriving after our Atlantic crossing and seeing red flares of spewing lava in the evening sky on the horizon!

It was easy in those days—following the breakout of war between Russia and Ukraine, new waves of the Covid-19 pandemic, and widening economic chaos—to conjure up apocalyptic scenarios. When we first arrived at the condo on St. Martin, it seemed grimly appropriate to me that the address was 13 Ocean Drive.

None of these harbingers of doom had any effect on Yves at all, which only further deepened my anxiety. He strutted along, telling a story to Stacy, as we followed a muddy track through mangroves that eventually opened on a white sand beach with baby-blue water. To the right, a few heavyset nudists were tramping toward the sea. To the left, a bathing-suit-clad couple and a family were spread on their towels. They looked at us—white-skinned new arrivals—and turned away. There was plenty of room. We parked ourselves in the middle of Happy Bay with fifty yards of sand to ourselves.

After I was dry from our swim, the sun became too hot and I retreated to the drizzled shade of a thornbush tree near the mangrove. Roosters cawed in the distance. The smell of rot mingled with the cerulean sparkle of the sea. The heat reflected off the hard-baked clay under my sneakers, reminding me of how vulnerable to the sun we would be on the deck of the boat in the southern latitudes. Even covered in sunblock, we would easily burn. The first three days we would be seasick too, probably puking.

Now that I'd seen *Orion*, the reality of the trip was sinking in. How had I come to such a jarring juncture in my life?

Casting myself into the center of the ocean seemed, at that moment, nothing more than a dramatic, useless *gesture*. Yes, I had long had the dream, but now I was sixty-four years old, soon officially a senior citizen. Had I waited too long? What was I *thinking*? I glanced back at the beach, hoping my wife and our friends would wilt more quickly. I wanted to get back to the air-conditioned view of the bay and take a nap.

CHAPTER 2

Limbas

My crush on the Atlantic first took hold when I was thirteen years old, sitting on the headmaster's porch at a boarding school located on a hill overlooking the ocean in Newport, Rhode Island. I was wearing tight gray flannels that ended above my ankles and a scratchy new white cotton shirt. While my mother talked to the headmaster's wife, I, a pavement-bound city kid, watched, dazzled as students—boys and girls—strolled down the sunlit fields that rolled to the one-mile-long beach below. When I learned the school, one of the first prep schools to become coed, also had a large oceangoing sailboat and an oceanography program, I knew I was going to do everything I could to get in. Though I had the grades—it was not an academically top-notch school—I would have to apply for financial aid. And there were several other boys at my elementary school in New York City who had already sent in their applications.

At the time, in 1970, my sister and I lived with our mother in a two-bedroom apartment on the sixth floor of the Bolivar, a redbrick building on Manhattan's Upper West Side. We had moved there when my sister and I returned from California, two and half years before.

The run-down 1920s-era building was still nominally

managed by its owner, Miss Ellis, as a hotel. It provided housekeeping service to some of the elderly residents, but the only transients at the "Hotel Bolivar" were the Harlem pimps who double-parked their candy-colored Cadillacs in front of the tattered canopy facing the park. They wore wide-brimmed fedoras and flared pants and boots, and bought their menthol cigarettes from Sam, a graying, hunched Mets fan who ran the newspaper stand in the vestibule immediately inside the glass front doors.

Opposite the entrance to the lobby, Mary, an Irishwoman with a patch over one eye and a cleft lip, ran the switchboard and retrieved keys and pink phone-message slips from their cubbyholes. When I got home from school, Mary filled me in.

"Your mother is out for an audition. She'll be home for dinner," she might say, handing me a raft of messages. "Be sure to get your homework done." On a good day she'd add a wink or a quick smile. My sister and I were the only children in the building, and Mary had taken a liking to me.

On the south side of the once grand gilded lobby was an area with card tables and chairs reserved for the seniors who were the primary residents of the hotel. They were mostly German and Eastern European Jews, many with concentration camp numbers tattooed on their lower arms. I looked at them a little amazed they were there, still alive in one piece, playing bridge.

The elevator men—Herb, a black man; and Burt, a pale, once-aspiring opera singer who bellowed arias going up and down the elevator shaft—wore brown uniforms with gold piping and helped shuttle the seniors to the sidewalk when they were going out.

My mother, then a striking thirty-six-year-old blond actress of some renown, and my sister and I stood out in the lobby, but we weren't *that* different from the other eccentrics who resided at the Bolivar. Baroness "Nica" de Koenigswarter, the aging patroness of jazz greats such as Thelonious Monk (whose well-known tune "Blue Bolivar Blues" is said to have been inspired by the hotel), lived there. A chiropterologist who worked at the Museum of Natural History rented an apartment down the hall. A professional clown wore his elongated shoes through the lobby.

The unusual mix of residents living at the Bolivar didn't faze my mother, who grew up in hotels. She was the daughter of Elizabeth Foster Johnson, a Southern belle, whose third husband was the German count Franz Egon von Fürstenberg, my mother's father. In the summer of 1935, my four-year-old mother, Baroness Betsy, dressed in lederhosen, returned from a vacation in the Thuringian mountains with her nanny to the count's opulent apartment in Berlin overlooking the Tiergarten, to find the manservants in their royal purple livery and white gloves busily arranging rows of crates and traveling trunks. Her mother, in a slinky Greta Garbo dress, puffing on a cigarette holder, announced they were going to America, leaving behind my mother's father, the apartment she had grown up in, and the Gothic castle in Westphalia where she was born.

A few weeks later, the countess, my mother, and her German Catholic nanny boarded the ship *Bremmer*. They eventually landed in New York, at first staying in a duplex penthouse suite at the Hotel Dorset and then, during World War II, as the money gradually ran out, in increasingly past-their-prime hotels.

My mother had supported herself as a model since she was sixteen, then continued to provide for our family as an actress. Many of her friends in the theater lived on the Upper West Side. She felt at home at the Bolivar and was pleased with her find—a sunny corner apartment with a view of the park for about $325 a month. The year I was looking at boarding schools, she rehearsed and then costarred in Neil Simon's *The Gingerbread Lady* on Broadway. Landing such a plum role was a reminder of the heady years in the 1950s and early 1960s when she was cast as a pesky ingenue in many Broadway productions and appeared on the covers of *Life* and *Look* magazines. But it was Simon's fame that put *The Gingerbread Lady*—and my mother's name—on the side of New York City buses. Her reviews were good, and her agent was calling again with offers. But the play closed five months after it opened, and she was back on unemployment and dependent on commercials and Off-Broadway work. There was often less than a hundred dollars in her bank account (I knew in which drawer she kept her blue Dime Savings Bank passbook, along with her rolled-up stockings) at the end of the month after paying for groceries, clothes, and school expenses. Still, she was proud to have managed to gather the three of us back together. She decorated the apartment with remnant furniture and the stand-up piano from the apartment on the East Side where we had lived before my parents separated. Ceiling-to-floor silk curtains were tied back by a sash. An antique silver cigarette box and ashtray stamped with the von Fürstenberg crest, one of the few remnants of her aristocratic origins, sat on the marble-topped coffee table a carpenter had made for her when we lived in Ecuador. Over the Christmas holidays she would sometimes throw a party and her friends, which included a Hollywood and Broadway star or two, and the well-heeled from the other side of the park would drop in to say hello or gawk at the surroundings.

Up close, our home wasn't swank. The radiators clanked and the window paint was flaking off. The "kitchen" was the size of a walk-in closet. Cockroaches slipped out of the drawers. My just-turned-teenager older sister was not impressed.

"I will never bring my friends here," she told me. "It's too embarrassing."

She went to a private Catholic all-girls school on the East Side, and she didn't like the West Side or the Bolivar. Plus, she had to share a bedroom with me, her brother, whose voice was changing. Between the lack of money (rent and tuition nearly always in arrears), my adolescence, my mother's prescription drug problem, and my sister's precocious socializing, it was a struggle. My mother was skittish and moody—maternal and protective one moment, regal and demanding the next. She once hit me in the head so hard her hand turned black and blue. She wrote this in her diary, adding with some satisfaction that for days after I would flinch when she raised a hand. Mostly, though, she raved at my sister. They would slap and hit each other, toss things—plates, ashtrays, books—pick up scissors or a knife, slam doors.

I was stuck in the middle. At the end of an evening, I dragged the garbage bag down the long hallway, past the blaring televisions, the marital arguments, and the smell of meat loaf, to the garbage cans in the rear stairwell. I remember thinking, "How long can this last?"

By the time I was twelve or thirteen, I knew my best chance

of survival was to leave the Bolivar and my mother behind. At the end of seventh grade, with encouragement from my sister (my mother wanted me to stay in New York), I decided to apply to the school on the hill overlooking the sea. It belonged to a different world, far from the crime-singed streets of the Upper West Side, the drug addicts and domino players on the corner, the war protests, garbage strikes, blackouts, and muggings that were a regular part of city life in those days. There were idyllic photographs in the school catalog of a student reading under an elm tree on a pristine lawn in front of a dorm, and another of the school's fleet of small racing sailboats known as Dragonflies tacking in a regatta. I had never sailed a boat bigger than a Sunfish, but I was hooked on the *idea* of sailing.

Like many boys my age, I'd grown up reading sea adventure stories about explorers, pirates, and whalers. We were familiar with Long John Silver and Jim Hawkins, Captain Ahab and Moby Dick, the *Bounty* and Captain Bligh. I was particularly drawn to stories about nautical exploits during the American Revolution. It was from books like Kenneth Roberts's novels *Captain Caution* and *The Lively Lady* that I learned about caravels and schooners, frigates and clipper ships—these tall-masted bulwarks of oak planks and billowing sails so vital to America's path to independence and prosperity. Now maybe I would be going to school in Newport, Rhode Island, an aging navy town and a forgotten jewel of American colonialism. Newport was also home to the America's Cup race for over 125 years. I didn't know much about it, but this competition conjured up a mixture of gritty rivalry, courage on the high seas, and glamor. To me, learning how to sail, tie a bowline knot, or tack into the wind were skills to be acquired, as American (at least in New England) as throwing a baseball or whacking a golf club.

As it was, I was accepted to the school, but it took me a long time to get on a boat in Newport. At St. George's School, I was a New Yorker, and I clustered with other scholarship urbanites, including my best friend, Jason. He and I had long hair, smoked cigarettes, drank cheap rum, and dropped acid (I was reading Ram Dass and Hermann Hesse). We listened to Neil Young, the Allman Brothers, War, Jimi Hendrix, Bruce Springsteen (Jason's favorite), and the Grateful Dead. At night we joined others huddled near the stone walls in the fields, icy and remote, drawing raw smoke from a bong, deriding the prefects, laughing boldly under Orion's twinkling belt. The waves in the distance shushed us as we crept back toward the shadow of the school chapel's Gothic tower.

In our tiny, separate dorm rooms, we piled furniture against our doors to stop the senior thugs from midnight hazing raids. It turned out there was a *Clockwork Orange* side to the school on the hill: a tradition of cruel hazing of freshmen and chronic sexual abuse on the part of certain faculty and coaches. If you departed from conventional preppy behavior or attire—your hair was *too* long, you preferred art to athletics, or, as one of my classmates did, you played the bagpipes or betrayed any remotely "gay" characteristics—you were a target. Your room was ransacked, you were beaten and "knuckled." One dorm prefect, a member of the school choir, with short bangs across his forehead, was rumored to have stuck a freshman's head in a toilet and a plunger handle up his rectum.

The sailing crowd, though, was mostly made up of earnest, local day students who grew up around boats and the elite kids who came from wealthy enclaves like Locust Valley, Long Island, and Greenwich, Connecticut, and had been lunching on turkey club sandwiches and iced tea at their parents' yacht clubs all their lives. They wore Brooks Brothers khaki pants and outsized Lacoste polo shirts and were given BMWs when they turned sixteen. Of course, many of those rich suburban kids were as drug addled and sloppy as we city slickers, but the sailing crew tended to attract the clean-cut, healthy, outdoorsy types. Freshman year I fell for one, a local girl who was smart but innocent. She had blond hair, blue eyes, long legs, and a cheerleader disposition; she wore L.L.Bean topsiders every day with no socks. She and the sailing gang had their own sailing lexicon: someone's uncle owned a *gaff-rigged catboat*; in the harbor there were *sloops* and *ketches* and *yawls*, some had a *boom-vang* and a *windlass*; every sailor tied a *bowline* and *sheet bend* blindfolded.

In the yearbook I'd check out the photographs of the student semesters spent on the school sailboat, *Geronimo*, in the Caribbean. There were my schoolmates Beaver and Alex tagging sharks, Lisa and Collin pulling up the mainsail, others clinging to the rail as the boat heeled over in a brisk breeze, gathering at sunset in the cockpit. It looked like fun, but the thought of spending several weeks in the intimacy of a boat cabin with a half dozen other students with completely different backgrounds and a lifetime acquaintance with sailing was intimidating. Not to mention the program cost close to $1,000.

So I pushed the boats aside. I played soccer. By sophomore year, I ran the coffee shop, a dank basement smoking room I repurposed into a French café, with tables, overhead shaded lights, a long wood bar built with the school carpenter (we served coffee and doughnuts and, if you were in the know, cans of coke spiked with rum), and a small stage for acoustic performances. I was popular, though a rough fit. Privileged but without cash. Athletic but not a jock. I was a percipient reader, an honor student, but also dyslectic, it turned out.

"Too many careless mistakes!" my English teacher wrote repeatedly on my essays. He was a young marine vet of patrician background who helped build an orphanage in Vietnam. He paced around the oval table in our classroom barking our last names in a jocular military way, pouncing us with surprise questions about American and English classics: *A Separate Peace, Lord of the Flies, The Jungle, The Ox-Bow Incident, Hamlet,* and *The Tempest.*

Feeling as much French (my father, a French Algerian, was then living in Paris) as American, I wore a bolero and scarf, and walked restlessly along the beaches, the rocky escarpments, and cliffs of Newport looking out at the ocean, imagining being out in it, listening to the foghorn at night, fantasizing about a life at sea.

At the time, sailors were making headlines for their solo ocean crossings and around-the-globe circumnavigations. These ruffle-haired adventurers, guided only by sextants and the whim of their imaginations, wrote about their existences on beaches in Tahiti and Mexico where they survived—with their lithe French wives and naked children—by fishing and cracking coconuts. In the '70s, beach bums wandering the tropics on old wooden sailboats were the equivalent of beatniks piling into a VW bus with a stash of mescaline and heading across country to California. It was getting off the grid. It was discovering an authentic way of living. It was, for me, a daydream. I had no way of getting hold of a boat, and if I did, I wouldn't know the first thing about what to do with it.

Truth was, I was still too much of a city boy with no nautical background. I was too erratic to focus on tying a sheet bend or rolling hitch or to learn to navigate with a sextant in choppy seas. I was too cynical to discuss points of sail (the direction of the boat vis-à-vis the wind) on the dock with Howie, the red-haired, freckled sailing coach.

And my blond crush fell for an equally ebullient classmate, a hockey star who also wore topsiders, the same kind as my heartbreak—soft-soled, with the leather bow laces left undone.

I spent my sophomore summer back at the Bolivar, running the elevator. Burt and Herb taught me how to bring the elevator to a smooth stop at exactly the right level with the floor, adjusting minutely if needed so no one would trip. The elderly residents cooed about how tall I had grown. I was a "young man" now, and the sex workers flirted and teased me. The pimps slipped me a dollar. An elderly lady on the ninth floor would push the call button and when I arrived she was standing with her bony, bare back to the elevator.

"Sonny, could you zip me up?"

At night I went out with a reedy, speed-dropping, professional backgammon and chess player who competed in all-night matches in after-hours clubs. On the weekends I went to Central Park and hung out at "the fountain" with the other long-hairs, jugglers, and musicians playing their guitars, bongos, and harmonicas.

It was the 1970s, and my mother was making the transition

from acting to writing. She had a syndicated column about the changing mores and evolving notions about beauty and behavior of the time. She went downtown to interview cultural icons like Andy Warhol or Betty Friedan. She was still acting, often out of town, occasionally on Broadway and sometimes on television soap operas. She was writing a romance novel. She was cracking open a new life, which would, a few years later, lead to literary and financial success and a new husband. But at the moment, it was still hard work keeping it all together, finding jobs, and paying the rent and tuitions.

That summer she had an operation (she never told me what it was) and had to stay in bed for a few weeks. When I wasn't working the elevator, I played caretaker, man about the house, and entertainer. In the morning on the weekends, I'd lie on her bed with my head on her lap, her hand idly combing my hair, as we shared the newspaper.

"How much do you love me?" she'd query me before asking for a favor.

I did not know who or what I was, but I pretended I did. I walked a thin line between the little I knew, the responsibility I tried to take on in the absence of my father, and the abyss. I would get too high. I would drink too much. I would lose it.

My junior year I was suspended from school for drinking and nearly expelled for my hijinks. I was caught returning from my dark-eyed poet girlfriend's room one morning. (She was a senior soon on her way to Stanford.) I had an accident driving the headmaster's car . . . at night . . . in a snowstorm . . . drunk.

Later that year, the faculty became alarmed when I was elected head prefect—basically president of the senior class.

They held a special meeting to annul the election. Voices were raised, but my English teacher who became my mentor—and by then the dean of students—and a couple of other teachers stood up for me and tradition took its course.

It was a cringe-worthy year. I tried to be both responsible and cool, craven and radical. I introduced an arts week to the school-year schedule and the option of taking a semester off from sports to do an extracurricular activity, and I graduated with honors. And though the headmaster wrote a letter to my mother threatening not to allow me to graduate if the tuition was not paid, he caved in the end. He didn't want to jeopardize the school's only admission into Harvard that year.

I left St. George's never having applied to the Geronimo Program or raised a sail on one of the school's boats. After four years living by the sea in one of New England's busiest sailing ports, the home of the America's Cup race, I'd never stepped off a dock and been on the water.

Author at St. George's

The summer after graduation, I was renting an apartment in Newport with two friends. One, Paul, had grown up sailing. His family had a turn-of-the-century Italianate stucco villa called Arcady at the top of a hill in Maine, overlooking a rocky cove. The family boat was a sleek forty-five-foot all-teak craft built in 1949.

For a prep school student, Paul was eccentric, a fellow romantic who had already crossed the Atlantic on board a freighter, lived in Spain, and wrote poetry. When Paul's parents returned from sailing their boat to the Bahamas, Paul was given permission to pick up the boat, *Limbas*, in New York and sail her to Newport.

It was on *Limbas* I first learned about sailing. Over the weeks, after work or on the weekends, Paul taught me and our roommate and good friend Steve how to tie a bowline with one hand, grind a winch when tacking, and steer the boat through the oncoming waves. It was exciting to be on such a perfectly designed wood sailing machine, to feel the adrenaline rush when we raised and trimmed the sails, and the boat lunged forward, heeling as it slid gracefully through the water.

It was strange how at home I felt at sea. I had no nautical or marine experience and yet at times it felt as if I and the boat were one. I'd stand at the bow and feel the boat's buoyancy pushing back against the water, the waves lifting her into the air, as if momentarily weightless, before she crashed down again into the soft sea. There was a childish joy to the repeating motion, a fortitude derived from hauling in the lines and manning the winches, an intelligence and self-reliance to charting the course. All of which Paul could do without blinking an eye. He had sailed offshore in storms, been stranded in fog and by low tides, and he could navigate by sextant. I envied him his knowledge, his independence, and his lack of fear.

That summer, our big sailing plan was to make the seventeen-mile crossing on *Limbas* to Martha's Vineyard. Steve had invited three other friends we didn't know. It was sunny with a strong breeze on the day we left, but as soon as we passed the headlands of Newport harbor and entered the ocean, the sky covered up and we faced steep six-foot waves. To my surprise, this only heightened my spirits and my determination to sail on. But Steve's friends became direly sick. They lay on the deck like rags, vomiting. After a couple of hours, we had to turn around.

I was deeply disappointed. I was desperate to get out on the ocean, to go someplace.

Limbas

When we returned to Brenton Cove (where the boat was moored in Newport) late that afternoon, the rough seas behind us, I told Paul that one day I would have a boat. One day I would sail across the ocean, perhaps go around the world. He listened to me with a slight smile on his face. He was encouraging, but I'm not sure he believed me.

My love of the sea went underground, but it was always there. It would be a long wait, more than ten years before I'd be on *Limbas* again, fifteen years before I bought my first small motorboat, and forty-five years after the failed crossing to Martha's Vineyard that I flew to the Caribbean with Yves to finally set sail to cross the Atlantic.

CHAPTER 3

The Captain

At the table that second night on St. Martin, after our plunge in Happy Bay, Yves told us the story of his transatlantic crossing, from France to Guyana, in a thirty-foot boat, with an inexperienced captain, when he was in his early twenties.

"We used a sextant," he said. "We didn't have electricity. There was a problem with the battery."

"That was forty years ago," his wife said dismissively, as if that made the crossing any easier.

I had heard the story many times before. It was part of who Yves was to me when we first met in New York—an intense, skinny jazz saxophonist who had recently arrived from Europe and was making ends meet as a house painter. His transatlantic sail was something I'd always dreamed about doing myself.

"Were you ever worried?" I asked.

"No!" he said quickly. He crossed his arms on his chest, like the successful builder he had become, and stared down at the table as if it were a map of the ocean he had once crossed.

• • •

Yves and I both loved the sea, but we were hardly experienced sailors. Yves had not sailed much since his transatlantic crossing. I owned a small motorboat and had earned a certificate from a sailing school in the Caribbean a few years before.

During the winter we had done research. Yves sent me a text with a link to yachtingworld.com: "How to Cross the Atlantic from the Caribbean to Europe: Everything You Need to Know." There was a picture of a young man at the helm of a boat with stormy skies and breaking swells behind him. "A return voyage from the Caribbean to the northern latitudes (of Europe) can be testing for boats and crew. . . . It is a very different proposition to the way out (to the Caribbean) . . . as the crew sails northeast . . . the temperatures are falling and the weather can be very varied and occasionally *testing*."

The author quoted Dan Bower, an expert on blue-water or deep ocean navigation. "We consider the passage (from west to east) to be heavy weather and prepare accordingly. . . . The first week is guaranteed full on, close-hauled in the trade winds, and life at 20–30 degrees in a big ocean swell puts more demands on the boat and crew. . . . Preparing your boat for everything from flat calms to gales is paramount."

Gear needed to be "lashed down," he wrote, and water entry points sealed. Emergency equipment had to be made easily available in rough seas. The captain had to be sure to provision the boat with extra fuel, spare parts, water, and food.

I sent Yves a transatlantic account I'd found from 2015 when five yachts caught by an unexpected storm sank or capsized about two hundred miles from the Azores. A young girl flung into the sea with her father died in his arms of hypothermia. Many others ended up in a raft or the cold water itself, plucked from certain death by rescue ships and helicopters.

The evening Yves talked about his trip, we reassured our

wives—and ourselves—that it was a considerably less risky journey now than in the 1980s. There had been updates in navigation and marine safety equipment: GPS tracking, rescue beacons, and satellite weather forecasts.

"Even so," I said, falling back on my worst fears, "last fall, several boats were lost in a storm crossing from the Canary Islands..."

"It happens," Yves murmured.

"Just the other day, there was a story in the news of a couple who disappeared in a gale—"

"Can we stop obsessing about this please?" Yves interrupted, losing patience.

• • •

The next morning, five days before our departure, I repeated what I had already asked several times before: Why hadn't our captain written to give us any details about our departure or the provisioning for the trip? We still did not know, for instance, what time we were leaving and how many other crewmembers would be on board.

"Why don't you write him?" Yves said.

"Why me?"

"Because you're the writer," he snapped. The truth was Yves didn't want to be seen as fragile, a bothersome worrier. He was grooming his buccaneer profile for the captain. I wrote an email saying we had arrived on the island and would like to meet, have a look at the boat, and perhaps have a drink. It wasn't until late evening that I received a reply.

The captain apologized for his delayed response. He

explained in awkward English—he was Greek—he'd had a busy day. In terms of provisions, he wanted to know whether we had food allergies and what we ate for breakfast. He was expecting us at 9 a.m. on Saturday, *the day before* our departure, for a briefing and to help load the boat. But, he added, he could meet us in the next day or two, after work, for a beer.

The next evening, just as Yves and I arrived at the marina dock, a short, lean man with a shiny pate was bent over some garbage bags in front of *Orion*. He lugged them away too quickly for us to introduce ourselves, so we called out for the captain. A moment later, he appeared on deck. The captain was in his forties with unruly hair; he was bare-chested, tanned, muscular, and fit. He had striking blue eyes and a friendly smile. For a moment we stood in the cockpit awkwardly repeating generalities. He casually mentioned a change in the plans: two members of the crew had belatedly informed him they couldn't make the trip.

"Let me show you the boat," he said.

He took us below deck into the main room—the saloon—where we were joined by the man we had seen outside on the dock. The captain introduced us to Nikos and showed us our cabins. I had my own in the bow, Yves and Nikos would be sharing one in the stern. The captain's cabin was also in the stern. The fourth cabin, in the bow next to mine, was being used to store extra gear and sails. While the captain talked, much of it directed at me (as if he sensed my skepticism), he casually reached up to the open skylight with his arms to stretch.

I met his gaze, then looked aside, catching a glimpse of the cluttered shelves above the sink, the potted plants, and the taped-up laptop and other electronics piled about the navigation desk. New age paintings his girlfriend had made of mermaids holding hands and leaping dolphins were hung on the teak walls.

The captain turned to a chart of the Atlantic placed under Plexiglas on the dining tabletop. He explained that to avoid a pool of still air in the middle of the ocean, we would head north from the Caribbean and try to ride the wind at the leading edge of westerly lows coming off the American coast without being overtaken by them and beaten by "thirty- to forty-knot" winds. Three or four days into our journey, he warned us, we would be leaving the tropics and would need to use our offshore jackets and bibs to keep warm in the evenings.

"Do you have autopilot?" Yves asked.

"Yes, but I prefer not to use it. It runs down the battery. And being at the helm keeps those on watch alert."

The captain acted out a stance at the helm, looking up at the sails, the stars in the night sky. "From 6:30 in the evening until 6:30 in the morning we will have three-hour watches, and during the day we will have four-hour watches," the captain explained.

It was only then I realized *no* other crew members were arriving. Initially we had been told six or more crew would be aboard. At the least, we expected an experienced first mate to be on deck at all times.

"*We* are the crew," the captain said, gesturing in a circle to include the four of us. No one said anything. Even Yves was taken aback. He laughed nervously and turned to me, his eyes wide.

"I guess it's up to us."

• • •

When we got back to the condo, I kept to myself. I had been uneasy from the start with Yves's selection of a captain and boat. I was used to dealing with established, certified nautical organizations, charter agencies, and sailing schools that had offices on both sides of the Atlantic. Lengthy, detailed itineraries were sent weeks before boarding the boat. When you arrived, young men and women in khaki shorts and polo shirts manned the docks. Captains wore reflector sunglasses and carried iPads. If they hadn't once crewed a racing yacht at the America's Cup, they aspired to do so one day.

In today's sailing world there's a quirky hierarchy. At the top, you have the legendary idiosyncratic pioneers of solo circumnavigation. These gritty self-reliant men who sailed relatively small boats with only a sextant to navigate by, battled fierce storms, and were out of touch for weeks or months at a time, captured the public's imagination. In 1967, the Englishman Francis Chichester, then sixty-five years old, was greeted by a flotilla of ships and a quarter of a million fans when he sailed into Plymouth Bay having completed the first one-stop sail through the Atlantic, Indian, and Pacific Oceans. Chichester was knighted by Queen Elizabeth II, and his sailing exploits inspired a rash of single-handed, cross-Atlantic, and around-the-world sailing races. Two years later, Robin Knox-Johnston, a twenty-eight-year-old merchant marine, became an instant household name when he won the *Sunday Times*–sponsored Golden Globe nonstop race around the world, the first of its kind. Knox-Johnston and his thirty-two-foot teak ketch, *Suhaili*, survived hail-spewing gales and two knockdowns (when the masts hit the water) rounding the Cape of Good Hope in Africa and Cape Horn at the tip of South America, the most fearsome stretches of ocean on the planet. He was the only sailor of the nine contestants to officially complete the Golden Globe. That was, in part, because Bernard Moitessier, a well-known French mariner who was sailing a bigger, faster yacht in the race, spurned fame and fortune and elected not to cross the finish line first in England. Instead, Moitessier sailed on around the Cape of Good Hope a second time and continued to Tahiti in the Pacific, where he lived for two years. A devoted Buddhist and environmentalist, Moitessier practiced yoga naked in his cockpit in the middle of the Indian Ocean and wrote in one of his books, *The Long Way*, that he gave up on the race because "I love to sail and to save my soul."

Moitessier's long spiritual journeys were outdone, at least distance-wise, by others. Among those who have circumnavigated the globe solo multiple times is the Australian, Jon Sanders. By his early eighties, he had eleven circumnavigations under his belt. At sixteen, Jessica Watson became the youngest to sail solo around the world, miraculously surviving seven knockdowns.

New races like the Vendée Globe and innovative boat designs of hydrofoil-assisted monohulls and trimarans have whittled down solo circumnavigation records to less than forty-three days—and also added more women into the record books. In 2024, Cole Brauer, a twenty-eight-year-old, became widely celebrated as the first American woman to sail single-handed around the world nonstop, setting a new circumnavigation speed record—approximately 130 days—for her class of sailboat.

On a different pinnacle, distinct from these solitary

sojourners, are the team racers. This buff sailing aristocracy includes corporate barons such as Larry Ellison and Rupert Murdoch, who spend millions having their eighty-plus-feet carbon-fiber, computer- and satellite- guided yachts designed and raced by macho, hypercompetitive captains—among them, America's Cup winners such as Dennis Conner, Jimmy Spithill, and the New Zealander Russell Coutts. Their crews of brawny grinders (those that handle the winches that pull in and out the sails) and strategists, helmsmen, and navigators are fanatical about winning the big trophy races. In the famous Sydney Hobart Yacht Race of 1998, less than half the boats in the contest reached the finish line; seven yachts were abandoned, five sank, fifty-five sailors were plucked from the sea by rescue helicopters, and six drowned. Most of the survivors came back to race again the next year.

Way below the deep-pocketed and glamorous ocean racing teams are the rest of us—the masses of recreational sailors and boaters with our dorky floppy hats, sun shirts, and beer bellies. Every harbor on the Atlantic seaboard has its weekend warriors who compete in local regattas, as well as a flotilla of sailors (couples and families) on comfortable traditional cruising sailboats and even more spacious catamarans, who spend as much time playing and partying at anchor as they do cruising the coastline.

Lastly, there's a dying breed of off-the-grid, do-it-yourself independents, some inspired by utopians like Moitessier, that still exist on the fringes of the sailing community. A few are temporary visitors, mainstream professionals who decide to take off a year or two from their office jobs and careers to experience the freedom and independence of a life at sea;

some bring their families and make popular video blogs to help support their new lifestyle. Others are more bohemian—shaggy, tattooed, hand-to-mouth seadogs who live more or less permanently on their boats and get by doing odd jobs. It used to be every marina had its hidden corner of these vagabonds, their ragtag, decades-old sailing vessels slowly morphing into immobile, barnacle-laden house boats. Today, sadly, these self-sufficient, sun-grilled sea gurus are being priced out of an existence that used to be almost free.

• • •

Our captain, whom I will call Dimitri, existed in his own category: he was an experienced sailor working as an independent captain on the margins of the charter world. His charter website said he had circumnavigated the globe once and crossed the Atlantic more than a dozen times. But judging from our first meeting, despite a certain intensity, he was more relaxed and spiritually curious (so his girlfriend's paintings suggested) than a hardcore racer or typical American charter captain. That appealed to Yves and me; we shared a more casual European attitude toward sailing. For us, crossing the Atlantic wasn't *just* about endurance and discipline. It was supposed to be a spiritual adventure as much as a physical one—perhaps even enjoyable.

Of course, safety was a prime concern, and we quickly learned our captain was less organized and with fewer resources at his disposal than your hyper-efficient American charter company. For instance, his website did not mention that he lived on the boat, which we surmised was about twenty years old. There were enticing photographs of other "available" boats, but his charter business appeared to be a one-man outfit with transient help answering a phone in an "office" in Greece. He didn't actually charge us that much—probably just enough to cover his transatlantic expenses. The online broker who told Yves about Dimitri said it was the first time she had heard of or used him.

I *had* confirmed by email prior to wiring my deposit for the trip that the captain had a satellite phone on board. Satellite communication has become an essential, if prohibitively expensive, way to keep in touch with people on land during ocean crossings, and it's the most important tool in acquiring accurate, timely custom-prepared weather forecasts. Lately, blue-water sailors with deep pockets or endorsements subscribe to Starlink, a satellite network that allows sailors to be in almost constant touch through the internet; they can download films, make their own TikTok videos, keep up their Instagram accounts (the young American woman Cole Brauer had over four hundred thousand followers on Instagram as she raced "solo" across the globe in the spring of 2024), and consult with teams of meteorologists or fellow sailors (more and more transoceanic sailings are done in a flotilla) about conditions. But our captain was old school. He was guiding us independently across the Atlantic. The day we first visited the boat, he emphatically told us that his satellite phone was only for emergency use and brief text check-ins with his office. He was vague about his access to up-to-date weather reports.

After the sudden unexpected announcement that we would be without additional experienced crewmembers, it was clear we would be entirely reliant on him and our own limited skills and stamina to get across the ocean. It was no secret that multiple night watches in heavy seas for two weeks or longer were enough to deplete *any* crew.

• • •

That evening in St. Martin, while Stacy and Pamela watched episodes of *Bridgerton* on the wide-screen television downstairs, I sat in our bedroom with my computer, checking the marine weather forecasts for the tropical Atlantic.

For decades, setting out on predawn fishing expeditions, I listened on my handheld radio to weather reports for the East End of Long Island. The mechanized voice specified the wind speed ("ten to fifteen knots") and the size of the waves ("one to two feet") in the bay. If the wind was over fifteen knots or the waves over two feet, I stayed home. Ocean forecasts were of another order. For the Caribbean, the immediate forecasts were good: clear skies, steady trade winds from the southeast at about sixteen to twenty knots, and six-to-eight-foot seas. That was to be expected. Farther north, if all went well and we found some wind blowing from the west, the captain said we could make the Azores in as few as fourteen days.

I scrolled through my old emails to find a link to the single testimonial I'd found at that time written by another sailor about Dimitri (after the trip I found many more). It was shorter than I remembered. "He is an expert sailor and a great human being," it read, or something to that effect. I reread the sentence several times and looked deeply at the photograph of this unknown witness—a thin man in his weather gear, standing calmly at the helm of a boat. The fact that the man belonged to a sailing club made me feel more confident, and I finally lay on the bed and turned out the light. A while later, when Stacy got into bed, she turned to me, her face puffy from the sun and masklike with worry.

"Are you okay with things?" she asked me.

"I'm fine," I said.

But long after she was asleep, I stayed awake. The look on her face unnerved me. Stacy is an optimist. She rarely broods and worries the way I do. She and Yves have the same outgoing, enthusiastic temperament. It was clear, though, regarding our transatlantic crossing, Stacy did not entirely trust Yves's assessment. She had not been impressed by the condition of the boat or the reliability of the captain. I worried she had deep misgivings about the whole venture.

We had taken a weeklong Caribbean sailing trip on a catamaran with Yves and Pamela three years before. The seas and weather were mostly fine, and the trip had gone well. The only hitch had been that I did not get along with our brusque, short-tempered French skipper. Yves, on the contrary, did everything he could to become the captain's best friend. (The skipper, in fact, was an acquaintance of a friend of his.) He was determined to be first mate even if it meant slighting me.

Lying by Stacy's side that night, unable to sleep, I had no doubt Yves would show no fear on board *Orion* and set out to ingratiate the captain with his sailing skills. With thousands of miles to go, it was easy for me, an anxiety junkie, to conjure up melodramatic scenarios. I imagined my fellow crewmembers eyeing my private cabin, sizing up my weaknesses. I pictured myself fumbling with a knot in front of the captain, or stumbling onto the deck besieged by one of my recurring maladies—insomnia, a bad back, cluster headaches, vertigo, panic attacks (or possibly all combined). It's easy to make a mistake, sleep deprived, at night while competing with other male egos to outdo one another, which is mostly what team sailing comes down to. If things go wrong, there's no room to whine and complain.

Left to right: Yves, Stacy, Pamela, author in 2019

At two in the morning, I was still awake with negative thoughts piling up, one on top of the other (a childhood habit). In the darkness, with the wind buffeting the windows, reality became distorted. Had Yves deliberately put me in a no-win situation? Given the captain's impatience to get back to Europe, would he sail us too far north? Most yacht captains didn't attempt the ocean crossing before May. To venture north of 35 degrees latitude in a modest-sized boat in early April was to risk being caught in a powerful end-of-winter gale—or worse, an outright storm. I pictured one of us at the helm, disoriented at night, letting the boat be caught broadside by a breaking wave and the four of us ending up in an emergency raft floating in the middle of the ocean. I became convinced a serious mishap, given the circumstances, was not improbable but inevitable.

The stories about maritime disasters I'd read and words of warning I'd received before leaving New York did not help my already shaky frame of mind. I had called Paul, who told me of an experienced racer who crawled into a ball of fear when they first sailed out of sight of land on a transatlantic voyage from England. The racer didn't recover and had to be left behind in Portugal. Another friend—also an occasional sailor—didn't mince words when I told her about the trip when we met by chance at a literary cocktail party: "You *do* realize people *die* crossing the Atlantic." It was the withering tone in which she said it that was so humiliating. Looking over a coterie of New York's publishing world, I thought, "There is no one in this room who would be so *unwise* and foolhardy to sail across the Atlantic with an unknown captain and a tiny, inexperienced crew."

I felt deluded to take on this kind of rugged endurance test only fully trained, fit mariners should attempt. I had met serious ocean sailors who were built like bulls and spoke like marines. I was not one of them, inside or out. Had I misled Yves? What would it do to our friendship if I were to back out now?

The next morning, with the wind whipping whitecaps on the outside of our cove, we went for a swim. I had been silent and distant, hardly talking to Yves, but after the swim in the rough water I felt better, younger, more in shape. I made jokes about the dangers of the trip. On the walk back to the condo, I took in the rugged landscape and blooming bougainvillea. It reminded me of earlier adventures in my life—treks in remote areas of Mexico and Guatemala, reporting in the Andes in Ecuador, entering Tamil guerilla territory during Sri Lanka's civil war; hitchhiking across the United States as a teenager. I told myself I was being paranoid about the crossing. Regular sailors my age did it all the time. I needed to get a grip. I had three full days before our departure on Sunday to assess the situation. I promised Stacy I would not get on board *Orion* and leave St Martin if I still felt uncertain. I had plenty of time to change my mind.

CHAPTER 4

Leaving the World Behind

Saturday morning arrived too quickly. Stacy and Pamela were packed and had ordered a taxi to take them to the airport to catch their flight back to New York. Before they did, Yves and I had to leave for the marina to help load provisions onto the boat. We had hoped for a final early morning swim together with the girls in the cove. But sodden, dark clouds skid over the sea and a sudden squall with hard rain ruined our plan. We said goodbye at the door of the condo. The bright light after the rain refracted against the silver rent-a-car outside and the palm leaves scraped in the wind. Stacy held me tight, our chests clinging together. She was openly crying, which surprised me, and she couldn't let go.

At the marina dock, we approached the boat where the captain and Nikos were busy tightening the turnbuckles on the shrouds that held the mast in place. The captain hardly looked up when we called out our good mornings; his bright smile had disappeared. As soon as we boarded the boat he asked us, abruptly, for our passports. He needed to clear us for departure from customs. The office, he explained, would be closed on Sunday. We looked at him bewildered. He had not told us to bring anything.

"I'm sorry," he said, changing his tone. "I meant to send you an email." He asked us to return to the villa and get our documents.

"Should we bring anything else?" I asked. He shook his head. "What about our bags?"

"Oh, yes, bring your bags."

Then he rethought the day's plans. "Do you have a car?"

Obviously we did. He would ride with us to the supermarket, he told us, to buy fresh fruits and vegetables for the trip. We would pick him up on the way back with our luggage.

On the way to the grocery store, Yves asked the captain if he could berth in the extra cabin where the captain had said he was storing some gear.

"I only need room to sleep. You could keep the other things inside." Yves said.

"The problem is we have a leak in the sail locker," the captain said. "I don't want the sails to get wet, so I have to store them in the cabin until we get to the Azores and I can seal the leak."

After we left the captain at the store, I turned to Yves.

"He forgets to tell us to bring our passports, we have no crew, and now the boat has a leak in the largest locker in the bow, which if filled with water in a storm could help sink the boat. What else can go wrong?"

"Let's not mention the leak to the girls," Yves said.

Back at the villa, we packed our bags, said goodbye again—quickly this time—and headed back to pick up the captain, who was waiting for us outside the supermarket without any grocery bags.

"I need one of you to come inside. I forgot my wallet on the boat," he said.

"Jesus," I said. I thought of the trouble we had encountered months before when we had tried to wire funds for our deposit for the trip. Our banks couldn't verify the captain's business account. I had to visit a branch office where a bank officer repeatedly warned me the account might be fraudulent. It triggered all my alarms, bringing back childhood memories.

"I'll go," Yves said, and he jumped out of the car.

• • •

On the boat, after unloading the provisions, the captain sat us down in the cockpit. We three crewmen sat on one bench, the captain facing us, sitting higher, on the deck. His voice was serious and paternal as he described the safety procedures. He showed us the harnesses and lifelines we would attach our shackle snaps to *every time* we were on deck. His instructions were bleak but oddly reassuring. His earnestness made me think of the sailing coach he had once been, talking to twelve-year-olds before taking their first spin in small day sailboats.

But even when Dimitri was being deliberate and clear, his English was uneven, and he repeatedly confused me for Yves. Nikos, who was hard of hearing, leaned forward, straining to understand each word as people walked by on the noisy aluminum pier behind us. We tried on our life jackets with their personal beacons that would signal our location to the boat if we fell overboard. Nikos and Yves spent a half hour repacking the electronic devices, which were falling out of their flimsy Velcro pockets. My life jacket was so far gone the captain went below to find me another.

Later, we moved to the foredeck. The emergency raft was stored in what looked like a large white ice chest. The captain pointed to two steel latches, which had a cotter-pin release mechanism. The emergency raft, he told us, was equipped with water, rations, and its own satellite beacon. But he added, "It's always safest in a storm to stay on the boat—unless it's going to sink."

After our briefing, we went across the road to a local restaurant for lunch. We talked about our nautical experiences: my boat near Montauk, Yves's transatlantic crossing, and Nikos's training at a prestigious French sailing school. The captain was pleasant and lighthearted. By the end of the meal, we were feeling more like a team.

"Okay, now we move the anchor," Dimitri announced after we had returned to the dock.

We gathered on the deck of the boat in the midday heat to move the primary anchor from a bow locker to one in the stern. It was essential, the captain explained, to lighten the load at the front of the boat in case of bad weather and rough seas. After the anchor, we passed more than two hundred feet of heavy chain, hand to hand, from bow to stern. It was slow, tedious work, and we were soon sweating. The captain, his back to the hot sun, carefully laid the half-inch-thick chain in a crosshatching pattern into the stern locker. When the anchor did not fit on top of the piled chain, he lifted it out again and patiently rethreaded the entire length of chain.

The last job was to pull the inflatable dinghy out of the water and lash it down on the foredeck. A small brass padlock locked the outboard motor to the dinghy. Frustrated he couldn't open the rusty lock with a key, the captain grabbed a crowbar and yanked, accidently snapping not the lock but the motor clamp lever itself.

"It was a cheap lock he bought a few days ago," Yves, who had jumped into the dinghy to offer the captain his assistance, explained to me afterward. I looked at the rusty lock still attached to the motor. It didn't make sense. He clearly had bought the lock three or four *months* ago (when he first arrived in the Caribbean), not "a few days ago." It wasn't the first time the captain had stretched the truth. He'd also told different stories about when the other crewmembers dropped out of the trip. These were arguably minor fibs, and his accident with the crowbar just an outburst of frustration and impatience, but I took a picture of the flimsy, corroded lock as if I were gathering evidence of a crime.

At the end of the afternoon, Yves and I headed back to the villa to spend our last night on land. The condo was dark and empty when we got there; by then our wives had already landed in New York. They had left crackers and fruit for us on the kitchen counter—a souvenir of our vacation. At dinner, in a local restaurant, the wind shook the palm trees back and forth. We bragged about our trip to the waiter and had too much to drink.

• • •

In the morning, after a gray dawn, the sun came out and the sea sparkled. A rooster crowed as the curtains shifted like sails in and out of the window.

We had a cup of coffee and drove the car back to the rental office. From there a driver took us to the marina. Along the way, we passed families, dressed up, heading to church. Other people gathered at bus stops and huddled to talk outside coffee shops. Teenagers played soccer in a dirt schoolyard. To them, it was just another warm, sunny day on the French side of the island. In the evening, their families would gather to eat Sunday dinner; they would talk about work and neighbors and love.

By this time, I had deep misgivings about our trip, but I did not want to stay behind in the picturesque world I thought I saw from the taxi window or return to my routines in New York. I was anxious but determined, ready for a change, ready to second Yves's enthusiasm about our trip.

After months of preparation, I was sick of thinking about what I was about to do. I was impatient to get on board the boat. It seemed the last twenty years of my life, increasingly riddled with hedges and caution, had unconsciously paved the way for an irrational leap. Even if the voyage were doomed, I had to get out on the sea. I *wanted* to be in its grip. This was what life was all about—discovery, probing the horizon. If I didn't make it back to land, so be it. Perversely, that was part of the point of going.

At the dock, we took a photograph of the four of us with our arms around one another's shoulders. To prepare to cast off, the captain designated to us (confusing Yves's name with mine) the lines and fenders we were to handle. Then he manipulated the engine and the bow thrusters to choreograph an elegant three-point turn away from the dock and the nearby rock jetty. A passerby threw us the last line and wished us a safe trip.

Leaving the harbor and breaching the open water, I convinced myself we were just going for an afternoon sail. The sky was a brilliant, friendly blue. The deserted white beaches of Anguilla lay to our north. As we drew away from St. Martin, the wind stiffened and the waves grew taller.

About two hours into the sail, the captain gave me the helm. It was my first time at the wheel of what now, suddenly, seemed to me like a large boat. She handled the seas in a stately manner, the impressive weight of the bow, fifty feet in front of me, splitting the waves as we heaved and fell.

It was a good feeling. I looked around, getting my bearings. In the distance I saw breakers, exploding balls of white foam where the ocean met the last barrier reef off Anguilla. I pointed it out to the captain.

"If you clear the reef without tacking, you get lunch. If not, you don't eat," he joked and went down to the galley to prepare the sandwiches.

The boat was heeled over, the wind steady and strong. I leaned into the wheel, pushing the bow a few degrees farther upwind. Astern, the green, humped silhouette of St. Martin faded into the haze. We were leaving land, leaving behind the "civilized" world and its problems, its wars and pandemics. Out on the sea, there was no sign of cataclysm. No hint of anything amiss.

At last I was feeling confident and hopeful. Any storms were far off, it seemed, way over the horizon.

CHAPTER 5

A Sleeping Whale

The transition is a keen one, I assure you, from a schoolmaster to a sailor.
—Herman Melville

The first boat I owned came in a large, heavy carton box. I picked it up from a marine warehouse in Fort Lee, New Jersey, squeezed it into my VW hatchback, and drove back across the George Washington Bridge with a bubbly, pent-up feeling in my chest.

It was the 1990s. I was in my early thirties, an uneasy time for me. My marriage to Stacy, barely begun, was in trouble. A torn-jeans-and-T-shirt-wearing archaeologist when we dated, Stacy landed a position as an ancient-art expert at Sotheby's and was soon running a department—and dressing for her new part. Between auctions and cross-country visits to collectors, her schedule was packed. My future as a playwright, once so promising, looked less rosy. My teaching job at the public High School of Music & Art and Performing Arts in Manhattan—the inspiration for the movie *Fame*—was challenging and inspiring but in constant bureaucratic jeopardy.

From the apex of the George Washington Bridge I saw the Oz-like city skyline jammed up against the Hudson River and, to the north, the Throgs Neck Bridge. Somewhere below it lay the flat blue water of the Long Island Sound. A few miles east of Great Neck, there was an isolated sandy beach where I planned to launch my small, blue inflatable Achilles and start a new chapter in my life.

I had done my homework and bought my marine supplies: a five-pound fold-up anchor, flares, life jackets, a yellow rubber-enclosed compass, and a whistle. I had stencils to paint the registration numbers on the side of the boat. I was determined to do this right.

An hour later, I drove through the busy town of Port Washington and on past open fields and the regal gates of a Vanderbilt mansion from the gilded age. Opposite the Sands Point Golf Club, I came to the remaining gray stone pillar that marked the entrance to a mile-long, potholed private drive. It wound its way through nearly a hundred acres of woods and swampland owned by a former New York governor—at the time being surveyed and cleared for development—to my in-laws' isolated, modest 1950s house on the beach, not a hundred feet from the water.

I pulled in behind the house and walked around to the small back door of the garage, separated from the house by a rose-entwined companionway. I stepped inside the garage and stood in its stillness, the sound of breaking waves on the beach muted by the cement-block walls. I was hypnotized by the display of utilitarian history on the pegboards and shelves, the tool cabinet and corner cupboard, and the scent of the room's woody, gasoline air. Firewood was neatly stacked against one wall. Ropes were coiled and hung on hooks, shovels and rakes were clipped by their handles. The hammer and saw, the boxes of nails and screws—everything had its place, function, and time. I glanced again at the large unframed painting of surfcasters hurling their lures at a stormy sea that Marian, my mother-in-law, had completed decades before when her children were still young and ran into the garage yelling with abandon to grab a life jacket or a kite before tumbling out to the sunshine on the beach. That space had a magic I could not resist. It was a place I badly wanted to belong to.

I pressed the button and the old garage door opener rumbled to life and the chain rattled when the door came to a shuttering stop against the ceiling.

"Glyn, is that you?!"

"Yes, Marian, it's me!"

My mother-in-law, a trim woman in her sixties, popped her head in the door.

"You're here! Have you got the boat?"

"Yep."

"Where is it?"

"In the box." I pointed to the open hatchback.

She came out of the garage with me for a better look.

"Oh, I see. It's not very big, is it?"

"Nine feet, nine inches." I tried not to sound mortified.

"Well, I think that's wonderful." Marian declared. "It's exciting. Now you can catch more fish!"

• • •

I'd just fallen for saltwater fly-fishing. Whenever possible on weekends, or after classes were over in June, I'd show up on the beach in front of the Goodmans' house just before dawn to cast for the bluefish and striped bass that regularly cruised in the shallow water at high tide. It was blissful to stand in the Sound in my waders, sometimes with a good friend, in the lurid, Kool-Aid light, as the dorsal fins slivered the surface, closer and closer. But even with the water up to my chest, there were too often many more fish I could see out of reach, churning the water farther out. I needed a boat—a lightweight one I could easily drag from the beach dunes to the water and back.

My in-laws—Marian, a watercolorist, and her husband, Edmund, a prominent surgeon and weekend golfer—were practical people who held on to their emotional life carefully, like teabags dipped in hot water. They were wary of me, the product of a broken family with a tabloid past. I was not the sturdy all-American they had imagined for their coveted youngest daughter. I was emotional and opinionated, prone to thinking out loud. I drank too much wine at dinner. My future was uncertain.

The first couple of years that Stacy and I went together on visits to Sands Point were an uphill effort. I felt as if I weren't entirely present. Stacy's childhood friends warned me, referring to Marian as a "steely battleship." But to me she was, at the very least, steady and dependable. The lack of hysteria in the household was a welcome relief. I could hardly believe it when I came down in the morning to find that Marian had set the table for breakfast: each person's utensils, napkin, and mug was in its place. There was a ceramic tub labeled "butter" and small jars of jam, the kettle on the stove was full.

I kept trying. It helped I could talk literature and theater with Marian. And Ed, the first Jewish surgeon on staff at Columbia Presbyterian Medical Center, approved of my becoming a teacher in the public schools, the system he himself had attended.

It was my love of fishing and the sea, though, that really got their attention. Much to my surprise, fishing to them wasn't something *other* people did, an embarrassment, or a waste of time. Marian had befriended some of the elder local fishermen who had been casting from the beach for decades. She admired their skill and praised me when I came back to the house with a keeper-sized bass.

"Look at that. What a beauty!"

Marian was equally enthusiastic about boats. She was originally from the Midwest and had come to the East Coast as a young woman to be reunited with her father (her mother had died giving birth to her, and she had been sent to live with her grandmother). He liked to sail, and Marian fell in love with boats and the sea. Both Goodmans went for a long swim in the Sound nearly every day. They were tied to the water. A stack of dusty, tangled old fishing rods leaning in a corner, the clam rakes in the garage, and the photographs of the Sunfish they once kept on the beach were evidence of how much it had meant to the family.

When I got the Achilles, Marian made me promise I would take her out for a ride, even as she expressed some skepticism about its size and seaworthiness.

That afternoon, after she went back into the house, I pulled the blue deflated pontoons out of the box and lay the rubber boat flat on the lawn facing the Sound. I inserted the plywood floor "deck" and used a foot pump to fill the boat with air. It took longer than I thought. The sun descended beneath the trees' highest branches and the tide emptied fast, exposing a plain of shiny black mussels and rock kelp at the water's edge. There would be no time to fish for dinner.

Sunset was approaching when I dragged the inflatable along the sandy trail to the beach. I went back to the garage to get the outboard. The five-horsepower Johnson engine was old and heavy. It had been clamped to a sawhorse in the garage gathering dust for twenty years before I refurbished it. On the cement floor next to it were the new lines, anchor, and gas tank I had bought and also needed to be ferried to the boat. It was an unwieldy, amateurish ordeal. I wondered if I shouldn't have been correcting my students' term papers or finishing an act of the play I was writing. Halfway across the lawn I stopped to rest, when Marian opened the sliding glass doors.

"Do you need any help?"

"No, I'm fine," I said, waving her away, but I felt I was making a spectacle. At my age, I should have been driving to a marina and stepping onto my powerboat—with twin engines—from a dock.

• • •

As the light faded, I hurried to get the boat in the water, the engine clamped to the transom, the gas lines connected. Finally it was done, and I clambered aboard. Sitting in the tiny boat was funny, wobbly, cramped, and wet. But I instantly felt at home and safe. I yanked at the starter cord, the engine came to life with a puff of blue smoke, and I headed out "to sea" while Marian waved from shore.

From a hundred yards out, I looked back at the view of

the long, deserted beach that stretched for half a mile to an estuary inlet. My wife's family house, with its weathered plank walls, was barely visible above the dunes. It had become a refuge for me, and I had become attached to it. At that time, there were only three other, widely spaced residences on the shoreline. In the late-afternoon light, the silhouette of the vacant beach dotted with bayberry shrubs and scrub oak retained a primordial, idyllic feeling. Seeing the house from out on the cold sea, as the eastern horizon grew darker, I realized it was not as secure as it seemed to me sitting in the living room in front of the fireplace at family holiday gatherings, with the old clock tinging by the stairs. It was a fragile redoubt, a delicate artifact that I feared would not survive much longer, not for me nor anyone else.

• • •

In the next two years, I put my blue Achilles inflatable to good use in and around Sands Point. In summer, Stacy and I packed it up into the car, with the outboard engine and the empty red gas tank, to visit friends in Cape Cod, Massachusetts. One spring break, I took the boat (in the car) south to the Florida Keys to fish for tarpon. Finally, one summer, it came with us to the East End of Long Island to visit Stacy's sister, Tonne, in the Springs. I balanced the inflated boat on the roof rack of the car for the short trip from her house to the landing ramp on Accabonac Harbor. I was headed for Gardiner's Island—long in my sights—three miles away. I made it there, but on the way back thunderclouds appeared. Rain fell and the wind blew hard against the tide, stirring up a steep, whitecapped chop.

The boat and I were tossed about like a cork. I came back cold, wet, and shaking. My sister-in-law's buff husband, who had just purchased the latest screamingly fast Japanese motorcycle, chuckled at my audacity and tiny rubber boat. It was, after all, a small dinghy. Most people assumed I was using it to ferry to a yacht.

The next boat I bought, a twelve-foot Caribe, was transported on a small trailer. It was a so-called rigid inflatable, with a hard-bottom, fiberglass V-hull, and a twenty-five-horsepower engine. The Caribe was still a dinghy, but a sturdier, heavier one. It took me out to Montauk point, the holy grail of East Coast saltwater fishing, a *fifteen-mile* bumpety ride out of Accabonac Harbor—where we had started renting a house a few weeks each year. It was a long journey out. The real test, though, was the back-breaking return trip at the end of a day, against the prevailing wind.

My fly-fishing-guide friends, who charged $800 a day to take their Wall Street clients out on their twenty-six-foot, twin two-hundred-horsepower engine powerboats, made fun of me. They asked when I was going to get a "real" boat. Other weekend mariners raced by, creating massive wakes to swamp me. The surfcasters on shore cast their heavy barbed lures straight at the boat for target practice. The four-to-six-foot seas around the rocky base of the lighthouse lifted me up and down like a roller coaster. Some friends thought I was crazy or foolhardy, but I felt safe. I pointed out that the Coast Guard used inflatables to *rescue* people. The US Marines, recreational divers, and commercial operators depended on inflatables because they were capable of carrying much more weight than an orthodox vessel. *Baby Doll*, as Marian sometimes referred to the boat, was like a shark-skinned balloon—she would not go down unless all three tubes were destroyed in an accident or deliberately slashed.

Sitting just a foot higher than the water, constantly drenched by spray, I developed a keen sense of the force and mood of the sea that enveloped me, and I stayed clear of the boulder-strewn, wave-dashed point where more than one guide boat was capsized and thrown ashore.

In the '90s, acres of bass and bluefish would rise to the surface each fall to feed on schools of anchovies; their tails slapping the water sounded like the roar of hands clapping in an opera house. After muscling into the maelstrom of boats to toss my fly and catch a fish for dinner, I steered home to Accabonac. In the cold fall twilight, I knelt on the deck floor with the extended tiller in my hand, lurching from wave to wave, my body drenched, bruised, and numb. It was a long ride, the remaining light mauve behind the reeds of Accabonac Harbor, and the sky dark when I'd reach the house—a rental or a friend's place—and slump into a hot tub, feeling as battle worn and tired as Odysseus. I'd swear I would never go out again, but I loved that boat and my forays into the sea more than life. I'd wake up in the middle of the night and go out in the yard of our rented cottage and pat the boat on its trailer, like it was a loyal pet. I would even lean my head against it in gratitude for having taken me out where I could not go and carrying me back safely to shore.

By the time I bought my first "adult" boat, my life had changed. I'd earned a master's degree in journalism and published a well-received biography. I wrote occasional book reviews for the *New York Times*. I'd been interviewed on public radio and was lecturing at museums and the occasional university. Along the way, I contributed articles to various newspapers, magazines, and quarterlies; and I was a finalist for a prestigious journalism award. In journalism I'd found a more concrete form of writing I thought I could master. For a time, I was invited to New York's literary dinners and events. I liked sitting at the same tables with authors and editors I'd idolized, though I rarely felt accepted or at home with them. I was still estranged, untamed, a naïve. My heart was still at sea.

What I yearned for was a sailboat, ideally one like *Limbas*, but I didn't yet have the patience, the time, or the money for that. Instead, in the early 2000s, driving back to New York from a stint of research in Cambridge, I stopped in New London and bought a fifteen-foot center-console rigid inflatable Zodiac with a fifty-horsepower engine. To me, it was a mean-looking, speedy boat. I swore it was the last motorboat I would buy—before switching to sailing. I was getting too far away from the water, I was traveling too fast, it was too easy to get places I'd once only dreamed of reaching. Six years after the Zodiac, though, I bought yet another boat—my first conventional craft that I still own today. It's a few feet longer, a gentleman's eighteen-foot, navy-blue center console with teak foredeck, trim, and benches and bronze cleats on deck. It's the kind of solidly built, classic boat that elicits compliments, not ridicule by the fishermen in Montauk. I had also obtained a mooring in Accabonac Harbor, with a pulley rig to bring the boat to shore. Watercolorists and photographers gaping at the scenic estuary at dusk would include my boat in their paintings or photographs. Apparently I was no longer an outsider, a quirky boy from the city. My boat, and by extension myself, had become one with the New England landscape.

I did not acquire larger, fancier boats only to catch more fish or impress my fellow mariners. Along the way my purpose had changed—or become more apparent to me. With each boat I was able to go incrementally farther out, to discover new coves, a larger bay, a different shoal, or a not-too-distant island.

For many years, Gardiner's Island entranced me. One of the largest privately owned islands on the East Coast, it has been passed down in the same family since 1639. Lying in the shape of an albatross between the two forks of Long Island, it has changed little since colonial days. Vast meadows, once pastureland, undulate between stands of virgin white oak forest. Steep ocher sand bluffs and hidden estuaries line its shores. Those deserted beaches once provided protection for the largest osprey colony in North America. The osprey in turn drew ornithologists to the island, including Dennis Puleston (about whom I have written). He helped confirm the link between DDT and the withering population of birds of prey in the 1960s, founded the Environmental Defense Fund, and pioneered the movement to protect the environment through the courts.

Then, as now, few people except family or invited guests are allowed to step onto the island, which is protected by security cameras and guards on ATVs. Old-time locals tell stories about being shot at; contemporary trespassers are vigorously prosecuted.

In my boat, I anchor a few yards off the beach and gaze in at the forbidden, arcadian view. At dawn I've witnessed thousands of birds of every type and size rise into the sky as one noisy cloud from an inland lagoon. I've seen fish blitzes explode in its bays. I've sat quietly as seals gathered around to eye me in an intimate cloistered cove. To me, this is as close as I will ever get to discovering a new land.

I've also motored farther afield, to Plum Island, Gull Island (a mound of rocks where the Long Island Sound plays tug-of-war with the Atlantic), Fishers Island, the Elizabeth Islands near Cape Cod, and Tuckernuck Island off Nantucket. I usually have my rods with me, but my yen to catch fish is not unlimited. My fishing buddies go on catching one fish after another for hours on end. Not me. Increasingly I went out on my boat for another reason. I had fished and explored all the lands nearby. What I wanted was to venture farther out to sea, to get into the deep ocean, to travel out of sight of land—one of the only places you could still go to experience nature in its full naked force without people.

Each time I'd go to Montauk I edged slightly farther offshore. One late September afternoon, I went out about twelve miles in a southeast direction in search of fin whales. When the long, rounded ocean swells lifted me up toward the darkening sky, I could just make out the Montauk Point Lighthouse behind me on the horizon.

I had not found any whales yet, but I knew to push farther out into the ocean would be foolish. The sun had already vanished behind the clouds in the west. There were no other boats around. I would just get back to Gardiners Bay, forty-five minutes away, under the final streaks of twilight. Any mishaps—a fish-trap line caught in the prop, an unseen log hitting the bow, a clog in the fuel line—could easily turn into a dangerous situation. I turned the boat around. A couple of miles from Montauk I rose to the top of a large wave and was coasting down its slope when I saw before me the massive head of a whale, its toothed jaw open, jutting straight out of the water. It looked like a mythological leviathan. It was, in fact, a sleeping juvenile sperm whale. As I swept past a few feet away from its gray skin, our eyes met briefly, and then, caught off guard, it rolled and disappeared under the surface as if it had never been there.

It's difficult to articulate the meaning of that sort of experience. But the same irrational, mystical impulse that resulted in my unlikely encounter with the whale at twilight put me on board *Orion* with Yves, Dimitri, and Nikos the day we headed out from St. Martin into the sapphire-blue Atlantic Ocean.

CHAPTER 6

Hallucinations and a Shit Show

Sunday, 4/3 St. Martin
N 19.56, W 061.24
2,509 miles to go.
20 to 24 knot winds, 6–10 foot seas.
First day at sea. Clear skies. Incredible sunset.

Going to sea is a kind of obsession, an addiction, which has its own rites of admission, its own repulsive tests before the salty, dreamlike elixir is given entry to your bloodstream.

I remember that first evening on *Orion*, adjusting my sitting position in the cockpit to avoid the dense, meaty odor of the boiling canned tortellini that wafted up from the galley below, where Dimitri was preparing our first dinner at sea.

It was not yet dark. The winds had lessened to a docile, warm blow. Our first sunset out of sight of land had come and gone—all but a skinny belt of disco light that gleamed beneath the clouds on the horizon. But it was hard to enjoy the scene, and I didn't want to eat. I grimaced as Dimitri doled out the pork tortellini floating in broth to the brim of my bowl. I ate slowly, cautiously, and as soon as cleanup began, I tossed half my sticky pasta shells into the sea. Nikos and Yves had seconds. Yves said he felt *great*.

"I loved the tortellini!" he told the captain, and bounded down the companionway to help him clean up.

At the angle we were sailing, washing, drying, and putting away the dishes and pots was a lengthy, awkward process. Meanwhile, since Yves and I were to share part of the first watch from 9:30 to 12:30 that night, I stayed on deck and took the helm. The breeze had picked up, and though I was tired of muscling through the peaks and troughs of the waves, I was glad to have something to do.

A while later, Yves came up on deck, pale and uneasy.

"Are you okay?" I asked.

"I think I stayed below too long," he responded. He looked like he might puke, so I reluctantly offered him the helm.

"Thank you, brother."

Staying on deck and steering a boat works better than Dramamine to steady a queasy stomach. Nikos, too, stayed with us, sitting quietly in a corner of the cockpit, his hands crossed over his abdomen. The captain came up on deck for a quick look around.

"Stay between 35 and 40 degrees northeast," he said. "Everybody okay?"

We murmured a subdued assent, and the captain grinned. He was not seasick, but he was tired. He had spent days preparing and provisioning the boat. He had to identify the sail lines for us, show us how to handle the autopilot and compass headings, which cabinets to store what in, the valves to turn on and off in the heads, how to use the two water-pump pedals at the galley sink, the bilge, the lights and battery switches, and the gauges at the nav station. He charted the course and prepared most of our meals too. Finally he was going to his cabin to rest.

"*Kalinychta*," Nikos said, wishing the captain a good night.

He was about to swing down the companionway, but I called him back and pointed at the tall, cumulous clouds scattered here and there on the horizon.

"There are squalls at night," he said, giving me an annoyed shrug. "Let me know if the wind gets over twenty knots." Then he went below.

Early evening, before a squall

• • •

Our shift began as a pleasant, warm evening with stars overhead. Yves, at the helm, was feeling better and chattering. He had become a talker late in life, always ready with a story or a burst of song. When he ran out of steam, he asked seemingly random questions: "Are you ready to buy an electric bike?" or "Have you read any good books lately?"

I wanted to engage, to help keep up the banter, but I was still nauseous, and I felt uneasy being so far out at sea; it left me dizzy and disoriented. I was seeing things too. When I looked at the thunderclouds in the distance, they shifted subtly into threatening shapes and monstrous figures. If I looked up at the stars, I saw a spreading red nebula forming around them, like the colorful clouds of gas in photographs taken by the Hubble Space Telescope. Having never hallucinated before, I dismissed what I was experiencing. I thought it might be an atmospheric phenomenon caused by being so near the equator. Maybe it was a type of fata morgana, the mirror mirage on the horizon that caused sailors of the nineteenth century to think they'd seen the ghost ship *Flying Dutchman*. Or had I just cut off the flow of blood to my brain by craning my neck so much to look at the stars?

I didn't mention the visual aberrations to Yves or Nikos. There is an unwritten rule among sailors not to voice your fears at sea. Also, I was intent on following a set of dark towering clouds with telltale sheets of rain beneath them. I pointed them out as they merged and loomed ahead of us.

"Looks like a squall," I said.

When the wind started to gust, I suggested we wake up the captain.

"I think it's okay," Yves said. "No reason for alarm."

"We wait and see," Nikos agreed.

I'd sailed through Caribbean squalls before. I knew how quickly they could ambush and envelop a boat. I'd once been hurled to the deck in a squall and seen other sailors on board badly injured and a nearby Catamaran dismasted. After waiting a few more minutes, with the gusts touching twenty-five knots, I couldn't help myself. I called down below for the captain to come up and have a look. I had to repeat his name several times to wake him. He came to the companionway bleary eyed, took one quick look at the clouds, said it was okay, and went back down below.

There was a silence on deck after the captain left. Yves and Nikos were annoyed and embarrassed that I had bothered the captain for nothing. Still, I thought I was right. If anything, I should've been more adamant and insisted he come all the way out on deck to see a second, more threatening front of clouds trailing slightly to the east.

A few minutes later, the first thunderheads passed harmlessly, scattering heavy drops of rain on the deck. A second wall of black clouds, though, swiftly followed. As the front passed above us, a cold, violent gust of wind tipped the boat at a steep angle. The sea rose into a froth. Before we knew it, a deluge of rain, thick as a waterfall, pounded down on us. We were enveloped in a raging whiteout with buffeting thirty-knot gusts when Nikos finally dashed below to rouse the captain. Dimitri erupted from his cabin, furious and naked except for his underwear. He barked out instructions in Greek and English to Nikos and me—though he kept calling me Yves, who was still at the helm. I was not wearing storm gear or a headlamp. Being new to the boat, in the dark, in the middle of a squall, I had a hard time identifying the lines we were supposed to pull or release. The boat was stalling and tipping this way and that. The captain became incensed.

"Yves!" he called out to me. "Release the outhaul!"

I hesitated, not sure he was talking to *me* and unable to find the correct line. So he shoved me aside and did it himself. At the same time, straddling the cockpit like an action-film hero, he grabbed the tail of the mainsail furling sheet on the port side where Nikos was at the winch.

"Bring the shit in!" He yelled at Nikos, pronouncing "sheet" as "shit." "Bring it in!"

Once the mainsail was reefed, the captain commandeered the helm from Yves and told him to release the jib sheet on the starboard side while ordering Nikos to take in the furling line on the port winch. I was left standing helplessly, not knowing what to do. I began to straighten and coil the many lines that were tangled like a nest of snakes in the cockpit. The captain told me I was standing in the way; he could not see the heading instrument. I sat down quickly, automatically, like a berated dog, and continued to coil the ropes, my hands going numb from the wet lines.

Soon the squall passed. The stars reappeared. The sea calmed. Dimitri, his voice more level and paternal, gave us a short lecture. We had to memorize all the lines, we had to wear our headlamps at night, we had to let him know *before* a squall broke. He returned the helm to Yves and he went below to make coffee. Nikos followed him to try to rest before his shift. Yves and I were left alone on deck.

"What a shit show!' I whispered to Yves. "Our first night at sea!"

"It's normal," he said. "We have to learn more about the boat."

"I warned him about the squall! Reef *before* you have to."

It's a cardinal rule of ocean sailing. You always reduce the amount of sail *before* you think you might encounter high winds or a storm. This is especially true before it gets dark with an inexperienced crew on deck. I was seething. I went on about the condition of the boat, the lack of crew, the captain's abrupt outburst. Yves refused to say another word. As far as he was concerned, there was one captain and you didn't question his authority. Yves's watch was almost over anyway. He handed the helm over to me, coldly, as the captain came up on deck with his coffee.

"Glyn, go below and get some rest," Dimitri said to Yves.

We looked at each other confused.

"I'm Yves," Yves said to him with a friendly laugh, tapping him on the elbow as if to say, "Hey, what's in a name? We all make mistakes." They guffawed like old pals and Yves went below. They were already forming a bond.

As if to confirm my fears, the captain sat down on the port side, away from me, leaning against the cockpit and drinking his coffee. I could just make out the blue glint of his eyes in the darkness. Braced against the wheel, I looked up at the top of the mast, slipping and sliding between two stars.

"Are you alright?" the captain asked.

"I'm fine."

For the rest of my watch we stayed in uneasy silence. I was sure he had written me off, that he thought I was incompetent. I wanted to tell him I was good at two things: reading the weather and navigating at the helm; that I had, in fact, tried to warn him and the others about the squall. But the episode had unnerved me. After witnessing his fit of rage, I was wary of crossing him. I was hallucinating again too. It was getting more intense. Everywhere I looked in the sky was a red lava-like glow. At one point I saw a lit navigation buoy, eight feet tall, glide by the boat and disappear just as it passed.

Luckily the wind was steady and the clouds were scattered enough for me to steer by the stars. Being at the helm helped with the nausea. I managed to keep us on course and the sails full until it was the end of my watch. Right on time, at 12:30, Nikos came up on deck to relieve me, and the captain took the helm.

I needed to sleep to be ready for my next shift at 3:30 a.m., but I was restless and painfully alert. I went back and forth between my tilted, hot, airless cabin, to the slippery couch in the saloon, to curling up outside in the cockpit—the only place I didn't feel sick. Dimitri and Nikos, conversing in Greek, went silent when I appeared on deck. Then they would speak intermittently in a whisper, as if I were not there. It felt ominous—the shadowy outlines of their bodies, their muttered conversation in a foreign language, with the boat now more than a hundred miles from shore, the water sliding by a few feet away.

I didn't know anything about Nikos. He had been there when we arrived, and he clearly had a different relationship with the captain than Yves and I did. Dimitri ordered Nikos around like he was a hired hand or an old acquaintance he didn't particularly respect. Nikos told us he was just another paying crewmember on the boat. He was from the same part of Greece as the captain, but he had never met him before. The story didn't seem plausible.

As it was, I was sun- and wind-beaten, dehydrated, seasick, and had been awake for almost twenty-four hours. I kept wondering why the other two crewmembers had dropped out at the last minute. Did Nikos know anything about it? If he did, he didn't say anything. Reticent and watchful, Nikos was difficult to read. As for Dimitri, after the onshore antics and the squall earlier that evening, I thought he was capable of anything. I kept going over a story he told us in St. Martin about being boarded at sea that winter by the armed crew of a Coast Guard cutter, his boat searched with dogs for drugs. I wondered if Dimitri and Nikos were drug runners. There were many of them in the Caribbean, off of Africa, in the China Sea—modern-day pirates of the high seas. Late into the night, I listened to their unintelligible conversation. I tried to interpret the tones of their hoarse voices. I imagined being thrown overboard. I pictured fending off Nikos, stabbing the captain in the chest with my two-inch sail knife (which I had left in my bag in the cabin below). I hoped Yves would wake up in time to help me when I was attacked.

I was being irrational, but we were isolated at sea at night. The thought of the unfathomable depth of water beneath the hull and the great distance to travel before seeing land and people again was unnerving. My sense of reality was unmoored. I thought about the tales of captains losing their minds at sea; of mutiny, delusion, and suicide—*Odysseus, Moby-Dick, Mutiny on the Bounty*!

It wasn't all fiction. Christopher Columbus's hypomanic, grandiose behavior was well documented, as was the mental disintegration of Captain Robert FitzRoy on Darwin's expeditionary vessel, HMS *Beagle*. I had just read about the unraveling and suicide of Donald Crowhurst, one of the eight casualties of the Golden Globe race of 1968. Peter Nichols, in his book about the race, *A Voyage for Madmen,* gamely points out that "normal people aren't driven to try to sail alone around the world without stopping." Among the Golden Globe contestants, two hardy types had previously *rowed* a dory together across the Atlantic. A few months into the race, they both dropped out, one of them breaking down in tears on a daily basis. Nichols writes that among the other solo captains, almost all had "a dark streak of introspection."

More than fifty years later, even the ever perky, optimistic Cole Brauer, with her online navigation teams and legions of internet fans, broke down mid-Atlantic, just a week or so from the finish line of the 2024 Global Solo Challenge race, crying and thinking she was not going to be able to make it. (In a later interview, she revealed having been a "blubbering mess" talking to her mother during the first weeks of the race.)

On land, preparing for their voyages, these men and women, like other serious ocean sailors, are capable, careful engineers, taking every precaution to ensure their survival. But once underway, a transformation sometimes takes place. Nichols writes, "Sailors ... when they head out upon the deep, the constructs of society soon drop astern and they are surrounded by shooting stars overhead, phosphorescence in their wake, and heaving shapes all around them in the sea and sky. It is easy, then, sensible even, to become afraid." And superstitious. Sailors still carry good luck charms in their pockets; some won't bring bananas on board, others prefer not to depart on Fridays. In times before regular weather forecasts, sailors knew their weather rhymes by heart—not just the one about a red sky at night but many others, like this one about a mackerel sky:

If clouds appear as if scratched by a hen
Get ready to reef your topsails then.

There were documented reports in the nineteenth century about ship crews suffering from calenture (heat delirium) or scurvy who, in an overheated fit of thirst and tropical torpor, flung themselves overboard and drowned. In those days, the meteorologic forces behind ferocious storms and deadly calms were not scientifically understood. The sea was a mysterious place inhabited by magical creatures and capricious gods who cursed sailors who displeased them. But today it's still common for ocean sailors to have imaginary visions; to hear things and lose their mental bearings (all symptoms, also, of dehydration). There are studies exploring why sailors, both in the navy and on commercial ships, suffer from far greater rates of depression and suicide than the general population.

That first night aboard *Orion*, as I tried desperately to sleep, I visualized the inky, dark seabed below littered with shipwrecks and skeletons. How many sailors became so disoriented they no longer knew where they were sailing to? Was it the ocean void that brought on their derangement, or were these men driven to sea by their obsessions in the first place?

At the moment, it didn't matter. What was apparent was that I had quickly become a casualty at sea. My first night on board, I was paranoid (I had to admit, in all probability, Dimitri and Nikos were not homicidal drug runners) and hallucinating. It was me who was not okay. It was my thinking that was becoming unhinged.

If this was day one, how would I survive until we reached the Azores?

Lying in the dark, I thought of FitzRoy, the admiral and brilliant meteorologist (the first to publish regular "weather forecasts") handicapped by his illustrious family's history of depression and mental illness. His uncle committed suicide by slitting his throat. FitzRoy's violent temper and depressions wore him down on his yearslong voyages with Darwin. Decades later, he resigned from the admiralty, and he slit his own throat when he was fifty-nine.

• • •

My thoughts turned to my father's family's murky history. There were rumors about my great-grandfather, a Syrian orphan who went to sea at an early age. I had read his ten-page letter handed down from generation to generation. He was not mad or (as his mother-in-law claimed) a murderer, it seemed, but an emotional cripple and an obsessive. His brittle, spiteful behavior alienated his son, my grandfather Arnold Vincent, a war hero whose personality issues led to criminal grandiosity and abuse. My father, too, despite his better intentions, followed a similar path. Many of my generation of the family have struggled with addiction and depression.

On my father's side, nearly all of the men have badly stumbled, limped along, if not entirely failed in their idiosyncratic careers. One cousin, a psychic and healer, accused his mother, one of my father's sisters, of "satanic," abusive behavior. My other aunt was sweet and generous but a pathological liar. One of my nieces, who was bipolar and sparkling and witty, committed suicide. Another, a lovely dreamer, also bipolar, lacerated her arm in an attempt.

I think of myself as unimaginatively rational—good material for an objective journalist—but that night on the boat I doubted my sanity. With a genetic pool like mine, I could hardly be certain where I stood on the spectrum. Certainly dashing about Montauk Point in a twelve-foot inflatable for years had provoked jokes from friends about my quirkiness and obsessions. In the privacy of my therapist's office, I had admitted to experiencing bouts of depression and suicidal thoughts. But I thought of these as aberrations. Didn't everybody have those moments?

At the end of that first day at sea, exhausted, I braced myself on the couch in the main cabin, feigning sleep in the darkness. I was watching the captain, standing a few feet away in his cabin doorway, illuminated by the red light of his headlamp, waving his arms around. What was he doing? Why was he standing there so long? Was he practicing martial arts moves? Was he going to kill me?

It occurred to me that he might just be putting on his bibs and a storm jacket, but I was consumed by my paranoiac hallucinations. Were they signs of an underlying mental condition I didn't realize I had? Did this chronic distrust and uncertainty, this personality that constantly expected the worst to happen, drive me in a twisted way to this boat, this doomed voyage across the sea? What was going on beneath the surface of what I thought I knew?

CHAPTER 7

Absence

When I was in my early twenties, one late night, high, I wandered into a crowded bar on St. Mark's Place with a friend. There was hardly any room to move, and I jostled a man in a leather jacket as I tried to get a drink. He spun around and grabbed me by the shirt, pulling me into his hard, lined face. He was strong, built like a boxer, a Native American with bloodshot eyes.

"Why did you do that?!" He stared at me, pupil to pupil. "What's wrong with you?"

I may have been trembling.

"Why are you so nervous?" he snapped. It sounded more like an accusation than a question to me. But he was still holding me, waiting for a reply.

"I was born this way," I blurted out. His expression changed, as if he recognized something. Then he nodded, letting me go and turning away.

• • •

There are snapshots of me as a toddler where I appear to be happy and well adjusted, but in others I look shell-shocked and distant. I'm not saying the circumstances of my arrival are entirely to blame for how I turned out to be, but it's hard to believe, DNA and martini-and-amphetamine-laced amniotic fluid aside, that the chaotic domestic situation didn't also play havoc with the atmosphere within the womb. By the time I was pulled out by forceps one hot July night, my mother had been put through the wringer.

Already twice engaged to out-of-control alcoholics, one particularly violent, she was barely twenty-one on an autumnal afternoon driving up the Saw Mill Parkway in my father's racing-green Jaguar, its spoked wheels glinting in the fading light. She looked at Guy from the passenger seat as he shifted gears and muscled the car around another bend, tires screeching—a leathery, masochistic perfume in the air. He was wearing calfskin driving gloves, his black hair slicked back, and he had a small, sexy scar on his chin. He squinted when he glanced at her, as if pleasantly amused by her misgivings. Stuck in the speeding car, she was half afraid, thrilled but also safe because her best friend from school days, Arlette, my father's much younger sister (already married, a mother, and divorced at twenty-three) was in the back seat.

"Hey, Fangio, sloooooow down," Arlette growled in his ear.

"Who me?" Heh, hey, hey—the laugh of a cartoon gangster.

"Am-beh-seal!" His sister shrugged and gave my mother a resigned look.

This was the early 1950s. My mother was wearing capri-length tight jeans, a button-down white shirt tied at the waist, and a pale suede jacket around her shoulders. Her haughty hazel eyes latched on to Guy, doing her best imperious Katharine Hepburn.

"Guy Vincent, if you don't slow down, I'll get out and walk to Poughkeepsie!"

"*Peekskill*," Arlette, in the back, piped in.

"On the way to Poughkeepsie, I met a lovely blonde Gypsy . . ." Guy started to sing, the little fingers of his right hand dancing on the dashboard before leaping ever so briefly onto her thigh. Guy was thirty-two; he could kid and flirt with Betsy as only the older brother of your best friend could.

"Oh, I give up!" She was blushing now.

There was an empty straight road ahead and a red light. Guy slowed the car, revving the engine and double-clutching between downshifts before coming to a stop. They relaxed, my mother rolled down the window, smelled the cool fall air, piles of decaying leaves swirling and shifting in the breeze.

In a few minutes they would arrive at the house—a clapboard colonial Guy had rented for his mother's weekends on the hill, with a view of the Hudson, thirty miles from the city. There would be a fire in the stone hearth. And Marguerite, Guy and Arlette's mother, would have coq au vin in the oven. It would be like old times.

Ten years earlier, during World War II, my mother went to the Vincents' apartment on East 54th Street in Manhattan after school and spent the afternoons with Arlette and her older sister, Suzel. The Vincents were French, from Paris, and before that, Algeria. They, too, had fled the war in Europe and were new to America. After doing their homework, the girls flipped through American magazines, trying on makeup and playing vinyl records. In the evening, my grandfather Arnold Vincent came home, and my grandmother often invited my mother to stay for dinner. She readily accepted because the

Vincent family seemed so warm and friendly; she didn't want to return to the dark, sprawling hotel suite where she lived with her mother, who was as likely as not to be out on the town, if not already passed out. Once, Betsy had to pound on the hotel door and when her mother, the disheveled countess, opened it, there was blood spilling from her forehead.

Years later in Peekskill that weekend, no one mentioned my grandfather Arnold, who had divorced Guy's mother, Marguerite, and was living in France with another woman. But Betsy thought Guy more than made up for his absent father. He had certainly grown up from the lanky boy soldier she had occasionally seen back in the early 1940s. His shoulders were broader, he was more confident, a war hero who had escaped the Germans and flown as a pilot for the US Air Force. Since the war, he had done well. He wore expensive Italian suits; he had an apartment on Park Avenue and a townhouse in Paris with a garage full of European sports cars that he raced on both sides of the Atlantic. She'd been at the nightclub El Morocco one evening and seen him cut through the crowd on the dance floor, without noticing her or waving, and disappear into the back room where the owner and select VIPs rubbed shoulders and played cards. But no one, except perhaps Arlette, seemed to know where his money came from.

In New York, Guy and my mother started dating. They went to the movies and danced at the jazz clubs on 52nd Street until the early morning hours. One night, outside the bar P.J. Clarke's, in the Jaguar, they kissed. In September of 1953, before starting rehearsals for a Broadway play, my mother flew to Paris to spend a week there with Guy and Arlette. Something happened. There's a photograph of the three of them strolling arm in arm by the Seine, my mother snuggling my father and looking down in secret thought.

Author's parents with Arlette in Paris

Back in New York, the gossip columnists picked up on their relationship, describing them sitting at a table in a club, "holding hands up to their elbows." Guy was described as a "playboy" and a "race car driver." Some said Betsy was about to jilt Franchot Tone, an older Hollywood leading man (and her costar in their upcoming play *Oh Men! Oh Women!*) who she was also dating, for Guy. Another reporter dismissed the French guy as just a flash in the pan.

But my father kept throwing charm her way. He popped champagne and sautéed crêpes suzette for her at two in the morning after they made love. You could see why he made the effort. She was a fiery, petite bombshell with a fancy name and a will of her own. They were a good match that way.

A year later they either "eloped" or went on their honeymoon—it wasn't exactly clear—to Acapulco, Mexico.

Six months after that, in April of 1955, Betsy gave birth to a girl, Caroline. Guy stuck around for a few months to help with the baby and then he was gone. Again. He had been disappearing more and more often.

Darling, so terrific talking to you.

My mother wrote to my father in October, after a transatlantic call.

You've had your little wife very worried. I expected you over the weekend as you said and then you didn't even wire! I thought surely I'd lost you to some tantalizing [sic] chick from Montmartre. Anyway, I miss you more than I ever thought I could darling . . . I hope you come back very soon, certain Kitty getting very impatient.

Opening night was terribly exciting and glamorous. Everybody was there from Noël Coward on down. We got very good reviews, but not money notices so don't know how long we'll last.

Guy had run into a streak of bad luck. He'd sublet his Park Avenue apartment and sold a few exotic cars, then they moved into a small, cozy duplex at the top of a weathered townhouse a block from the East River. When his checks started to bounce, he told my mother not to worry, he was on the verge of signing a lucrative contract. My mother, too, was optimistic. She hoped the next play would be a long-running hit. Any day now, their worries would end.

But on this trip, my father's happy-go-lucky composure cracked. He wrote a letter from Paris saying he had two weeks to come up with $2,000 or he would be thrown in jail. His bad news was beginning to pile up. The year before, he had arrived late to Acapulco without the divorce papers from his first wife, Gael, and the marriage ceremony was canceled. My mother, deeply hurt, jilted as it were at the altar with her vows memorized, instructed her mother to inform the press that they had eloped earlier in the year and were on their honeymoon. The dailies obliged with one headline announcing "Betsy Has a Guy and He's Her Husband."

Now Guy was absent for an opening night on Broadway.

The play, written by Enid Bagnold, was called *The Chalk Garden*. In it my mother played an icy teenage arsonist, one of a cast of "mad" upper-crust characters detached from reality. "Miss Bagnold . . . sees how far they have departed from sanity by indulging their egotism as privileged people," one critic wrote.

My mother—nicknamed "Madcap Betsy" by columnists—had a flaw or two herself. She'd been fired from *Oh Men! Oh Women!* for spiking the drink of the star, Tony Randall, and kicking another actor in the shins for upstaging her. She shared my father's disdain for conventional mores and behavior; though they both had a preternatural talent for hanging out in high society with interesting personalities, neither had attended a New England college or been raised in a hidebound clubby milieu. They both enjoyed being "bad"—good fodder for the tabloids. She was unhappy but still playful when, a few weeks later, my father missed his entrance cue again.

Darling, I expected you all day yesterday—if you can't come can't you let us know? It's no fun to look forward and look forward—and then nothing! You could at least write one letter! I hope you are alright. . . . The play is going marvelously except we have a beast of a stage manager. I'm afraid I'm going to get in trouble again unless you come back very soon. You know how I am without my ration—Well, my sweet, I suppose you are not lacking for that anyway. I love you. Your still faithful wife, xxx Betsy. P.s. The baby got her crib . . .

Betsy was paying the rent. She was taking care of their newborn daughter. She was getting the baby to the doctor for inoculations, finding a sitter when our grandmother couldn't be there, buying furniture, having the apartment painted, paying my father's overdue parking tickets, making guest appearances on daytime television shows like *Strike It Rich* and then performing every night on stage.

She'd been coping with dysfunction and instability since she was a child in Berlin. Formally addressed as "countess" by servants and visitors even as a toddler, she was nevertheless potty trained by being locked in a pitch-black room. When she was sick, the family physician instructed her to eat her own vomit. Her parents didn't seem to notice. They were distracted by a family feud: the count was fighting his mother and younger brother for control of the Fürstenberg estates. It seems the count had spent too much time visiting the bohemian salons in Paris (where he was painted by Tamara de Lempicka) and entertaining his American fiancée on the Riviera and not enough time managing the family holdings.

It was a long protracted legal battle, and my mother and the nanny were often confined to the *kinderzimmer* (nursery) while the count and countess ate nearly silent meals in the dining room, surrounded by fading oil portraits and glimmering silver candlesticks. In the morning, when my mother and her nanny went for their walk in the Tiergarten, the tall, slim count would wave from the library window while the countess left soon after in a chauffeured car with a man the nanny described in a letter to my mother as "a muscular blond." She went on, "I do not know why your father allowed this."

At the time, the Nazis were taking over Germany. My grandparents' good friends, the American Consul General George S. Messersmith and his wife, who lived downstairs from them and had tried to warn Washington about Adolf Hitler, had been transferred to another post. Messersmith had already gotten a visa for Albert Einstein, and now many other important Jewish families in industry and finance were emigrating. There was fear and growing alarm in the air. The impossible was happening. It was time to leave.

After her mother divorced her father in 1935, my mother spent even more time alone, traveling with her nanny while her distracted mother searched the Riviera for another European blue blood to wed.

Before and after the war, my mother crossed the Atlantic more than ten times to meet her mother in Venice or Monaco, to work as a model in Paris, or to return to school in New York. These Atlantic crossings weren't about the ocean or the weather or confronting anything essential about oneself. For my mother and grandmother, when she was on board, it was about acquiring a first-class ticket and a seat at the captain's table. They lived out of their embossed traveling trunks—in which they carried their world with them to the next destination.

When my grandmother didn't find a suitably wealthy husband, her drinking spiraled out of control. In New York, she put Betsy to work, first as an eight-year-old ballet dancer and then as an aspiring figure skater and later, with more success, as a teenage model and actress.

In July of 1950, a bevy of reporters waited dockside in New York for my mother, then nineteen, to descend the plank after she returned from a working vacation in Italy. The photographers had her sit on her trunk, with her legs crossed, and wave at the camera.

A successful *Elle* cover model as a teenager in Paris, she had landed a small part in *Women Without Names*, an Italian film about women in a refugee camp after World War II. The role helped catapult her to the cover of *Look* magazine and a photo essay with Stanley Kubrick. Journalists were impressed that a "society girl" had a paying job. A cover story in *Life* magazine followed the next year when she was cast and

received good reviews in the Philip Barry Broadway play *Second Threshold*. "The most promising young actress of the year," one critic wrote. She was flown to Hollywood, California, for movie studio screen tests.

Poolside, she met Conrad "Nicky" Hilton Jr., a hotel chain scion on the bounce from his marriage to Elizabeth Taylor. The attraction was instant; Betsy and Hilton were soon engaged. But instead of marrying or making movies, my mother made more tabloid headlines when she dumped Hilton, who had beat her up and was plying her with tranquilizers and amphetamines (initiating a lifelong habit).

My mother returned to New York determined to continue acting on stage. She studied with Herbert Berghof (now the HB Studio), landed the plum role in *Oh Men! Oh Women!*, and remet Guy. At that time, in the glow of his financial success and the familial hearth in Peekskill, Guy seemed both dashing and capable, fun and reassuring. By the autumn of 1955, though, he had lost his shine; he was less Cary Grant, more Robert Mitchum, an evasive missing husband, my mother's dark-eyed French Algerian lothario.

> *My darling Guy, This celibate life is killing me. I am quite alone in our large bed—and in a "stepchild" state of mind. I am wondering quite seriously, if you have not deserted me. You must tell me, you know, immediately, if you have or when you do. . . . I don't understand if you do love me why you haven't the time to write—a word. . . . You seem very far away, darling, and I need you. . . . The play is going marvelously and the baby is indescribable. My only two joys at the moment. I love you, B.*

My father said he was still *madly* in love with her. But he did not explain exactly why he was away, stuck in Europe, North Africa, someplace else. He had legal and financial difficulties. His *American* passport had expired or been confiscated. He said he might get back into the United States via Cuba using his *French* passport. Then he changed his mind and, in late November, he wrote to say he was taking a job in Paris. My mother wrote back, in pencil, from backstage before a Saturday matinee on a leftover sheet of hotel stationary.

> *Well darling, missing you is getting to be like an incurable desease [sic]—incurable because you never come back to cure me. After your letter . . . saying you were taking the job in Paris Dec 1st I feel downright ill. Maybe you just don't feel like I do. But I don't think I can stand it. . . . I'm about to burst into tears for about the tenth time since last night and your wife—so I'll not bore you further—must put on the war paint now anyway xxxxx Betsy P.s. I had a terrible nightmare—I wouldn't see you till spring. If you let that come true I shall never forgive you.*

At some point that winter my father made it back to New York. He was there for my sister's christening in the spring of 1956—there's a photograph as proof—but I don't know when he arrived or how long he stayed. It wasn't more than a few months before my parents were again apart and my mother's refrain returned. That July she wrote to him:

Darling . . . Please, please come back—it's been so awfully long—I miss you and I want you here next to me—broke or not broke. We'll work out things together.

After being away for most of the past year and a half, he returned to the States in October 1956 and stayed for the winter.

In March of 1957, they gave a small dinner party in their attic apartment near the river. Actors Christopher Plummer and his pregnant fiancée, Tammy Grimes, were there. Theodore Bikel, a champion of the civil rights movement, who later founded the Newport Folk Festival, played the guitar late into the night accompanied by Josephine Premice, the Haitian American actress who starred later that year with Lena Horne on Broadway in *Jamaica*. My father, adept at sauces and soufflés, cooked up a French delectation. The party went into the early morning hours.

The next day, while Guy and Caroline napped, my mother, wallowing in domestic bliss, baked an apple pie. She was pleased the dinner had been a success. Only twenty-five, she had left behind the Hollywood scene and the Riviera clique of European aristocrats she had been raised among. Instead, she was creating a new circle of friends from her fellow actors and artists (some of whom she would remain close to for life). While her royal cousins and half siblings (her father remarried and had two children by Gloria Rubio; one, Dolores von Furstenberg, having famously married her stepbrother Patrick Guinness) sashayed from one celebrated fete to another in Paris, London, and Monaco, my mother had been working on stage in New York for several years, playing roles opposite some of the leading actors of her time.

Her moment of tranquility in the warm kitchen with a gray snow-threatening sky outside, however, was short-lived. While the pie was still in the oven, the downstairs front doorbell rang. My mother pushed the buzzer without asking who it was. When she hung her head over the stairwell balustrade—it was a four-flight walk-up—she expected to see a friend, but it was two plain-clothed policemen. They were there to collect on some neglected department store bills. But that was, it turned out, the least of my parents' problems.

Three days later, my father stood in front of the New York Supreme Court Justice Thomas F. Murphy and pled guilty to a more serious criminal charge, one he had kept secret from my mother almost from the start of their relationship. Five years before, in June of 1952, my father and his business, the American Refiner's Corporation, on East 42nd Street, received a letter from the US Bureau of Customs that two boxes on their way to Europe had been seized at Idlewild Airport. Labeled as "costume jewelry," the boxes were found to contain 133 pounds of twenty-four-carat gold strips. Almost a year later, my father and three others were indicted for smuggling gold out of the United States, a federal crime at the time. The scheme had been going on for years and, newspapers reported, amounted to millions of dollars in profit.

Released on bail, the lead defendant, a former boxing referee, fled across the border to Mexico. It took the authorities four more years to track him down and bring my father to federal court in downtown Manhattan to face the charges.

One Wednesday morning, while my mother read the newspapers in bed, Guy, accompanied by his lawyer, went to court and pled guilty. He had expected a suspended sentence and probation. He'd told my mother he'd be back that afternoon. Instead, the judge sentenced him to a prison upstate.

Dressed in a tailored suit and Italian shoes, and with a silk scarf in his breast pocket, he was taken directly from the courtroom to the Manhattan detention center, known as the Tombs. A few days later, on a snowy afternoon, he was transported to a federal facility near Danbury, Connecticut. It was almost dark when he emerged from a prison van, his hands cuffed. For a moment, before being ushered into the locked facility, he glanced up at the wooded hilltop prison complex surrounded by razor wire. He wrote to my mother the next day:

> *It's full of snow and I couldn't see much, but it might be very nice with good weather. I'm not supposed to have visits for 2 weeks but in view of your condition and the fact you have to come from N.Y. I might get a special permission. . . . As soon as you receive this send me $10.00 by Western Union so that I can have it by Wednesday. . . . I miss you more and more my sweet. It's going to be awfully long. I'll write more Sunday.*
>
> *All my love, ever, Guy.*
> *Guy Vincent 12814*

My mother was left alone again with her toddler in the top-floor walk-up on 52nd Street. The rent was past due. She was out of work. And it was going to be harder to get her daughter and the groceries up the stairs now that she was pregnant again. This time, with me.

CHAPTER 8

Containment

*Being in a ship is being in a jail
with the chance of being drowned.*
—Samuel Johnson

Boat cabins have been unfavorably compared to prison cells. In general, they are smaller. My teak-walled cabin on board *Orion* was luxurious, about eight feet long by four feet wide at its broadest. Most of that was my bed, which on a boat is called a berth. There was a skinny closet for gear and a head (bathroom) on the outer side of the cabin, along with a long six-inch-wide shelf above the berth where I stored shirts, shorts, gloves, underwear, socks, two paperback books, cell phone, GPS, pens, sail knife, headlamp, my journal, and a "heart rock" Stacy had slipped into my bag.

A small porthole gave me a disconcerting water-level view of the waves outside pounding the side of the boat, separated from my bed by about an inch of fiberglass. The hatch in the ceiling above my knees did not show the sky but the inside of the dingy, lashed down on the deck above me. At the worst of times, it felt like I was sleeping in a damp coffin.

As it was, the first two days at sea I was too seasick to spend more than a few minutes at a time in my cabin. I'd dash in to get more sunblock or use the head. It wasn't until the third day that I was accustomed to being below deck. When the boat was sailing in moderate seas it was possible to keep the cabin dry and orderly. My berth even felt cozy at times, when I was tucked into my sleeping bag at night, reading a book by the LED reading lamp, the waves rocking me to sleep. I felt contained and safe.

The main challenge, with the brisk trade winds hitting us sideways and the bow crashing through eight-foot seas, was getting up and moving around.

Ambulating in a boat tilted at 15 to 25 degrees is like being an acrobat or a spider. You try to gain three anchor-holds, with hands, feet, elbows, or back braced against something solid before you endeavor to go anywhere or do anything (that constant muscular strain contributed to my losing ten pounds during the trip).

Preparing for my night watch at 3:30 a.m. could take a long time. After rooting around on my shelf for a dry pair of socks or a not-too-smelly undershirt, I'd stand with my back against the downwind side of the cabin and my feet rooted against the toeboard of the upwind side. With one hand I reached out for the closet door and yanked while my other hand grasped the bed board. In one quick movement I would push forward, grab a thin Polartec top or vest from a hanger, and slam back against the downwind cabin wall holding the piece of clothing like a trophy. Using gravity to hold me in place against the wall, I'd put it on, followed by my socks, pants, boots, and various layers of clothes, ending with my damp storm jacket, life vest, and lifeline shackle, which hung on a hook behind the door. Inevitably while getting dressed the boat, hit by a wave or released by a sudden drop in wind or a turn at the helm, would shift suddenly and throw me violently against the opposite wall or the bathroom door. This happened to me repeatedly, like a pinball slammed by a drunk teenager.

To actually use the bathroom (because of the extreme tilt of the boat, water overflowing from the shower drain, the toilet, or the sink sloshed about your feet), much less to make a cup of coffee (a luxury) or dunk a teabag in hot water and bring it and a piece of buttered bread to the main cabin table, meant dozens of orchestrated moves so tedious and hazardous that more often than not we did without. It turned out, a quick piss sitting down, a gulp of warm water from a nearly empty plastic bottle, and a dry cracker were enough to get by on.

Once again I questioned what I was doing, at my age, in such uncomfortable, demanding circumstances. What was it with this boat thing? This need to test myself against the elements? As other blue-water sailors have mused, there is a paradoxical freedom that comes with being contained on a boat. And the rougher the weather, the more focused your energy, the more liberated you feel.

The need to focus on the little things, the practical realities, keeps the larger questions and doubts at bay. As much as I may have questioned my ability to accomplish the smallest tasks—locking on a tight life jacket, sleep-deprived, at night in a gale can be a challenge—I *had* to get it done. I could *not* let the rest of the crew down. We were, each one of us, responsible to see that the boat remained afloat and arrived safely, one day, at its destination. By the end of the second day on board, that prerequisite had helped restore my mental equilibrium, and I realized whether I liked them or not, whoever Nikos and Dimitri might be, I needed them and I wanted to belong to the team. I *had* to be on time to relieve a crewmate on deck. I *had* to help us get through the night to reach the morning. My entire being depended on being present and reliable. (I had long ago determined not to repeat the sins of my father.)

Fully outfitted, I moved ponderously across the dark main cabin and climbed the companionway unsure of what would greet me as I stepped out of the womb of the boat and into a night that did not end. Whether the sea was serene as a lullaby or bitterly wild, the first touch of the cool salty breeze on my cheeks made me come alive. I greeted my tired crewmates on deck, ready to take hold of the helm and keep the boat upright and pointed in the right direction.

• • •

Everything at sea, where apparently there is no one place to be, is about location, being in the crosshairs of the invisible lines called longitude and latitude. It's all about where you are in space and time, the compass bearing of your destination and that constant variable—the wind.

Each morning, after our night watches were over, Yves and I would sit down at the table in the main cabin, unfold our chart of the Atlantic Ocean and, using our GPS coordinates, pinpoint our location with a black ink *X*. We used a ruler to draw a line from yesterday's location to where we were now. Not unlike idle convicts counting days in their cells, we counted the miles, demarking how far we had come—and survived—and how long before we would walk on land again. The joy of being at sea was paradoxically balanced by the nostalgia for terra firma. Without arrival, the voyage lost its meaning.

When you're sailing in the middle of the ocean, the distance traveled is often hazy and the miles that remain are uncertain. You may count the degrees of longitude and latitude on the sides of the chart, but you never know precisely how far you have left to go and how long it could take to get there. You might have to tack hundreds of miles to avoid a storm. The wind could die, leaving the boat idle for days. The captain might miscalculate. A sail could rip. A wire buried in a locker or way up in the mast could short-circuit, knocking out your instruments. A pump could fail. Or a shipping container with new Porsches inside—one of hundreds of containers lost from a transport ship burned and wrecked off the Azores just before our departure—floating just beneath the waves, might stab a hole in the hull.

As we looked at the chart, the expanse of mysterious blue space between the X on our current location and the dots of the islands of the Azores across the ocean expanded and contracted depending on the progress we were making. The weather, the set of the sails, the skill of the captain and crew— each element contributed to the mood on board and the confidence we felt. It was a mix that changed from day to day, if not hour by hour. The nights were the most daunting. But even in darkness, if all was in equilibrium, the sea cradled *Orion*, the wind filled the sails, and the boat carried us safe and dry toward our destination. When morning finally arrived, our boat was a magical place to be.

At the chart table, Yves gloated over our progress and smacked his hand down triumphantly. His eyes glimmered with pride; we high-fived. We were sailing across the *fucking* Atlantic Ocean! We had escaped our measly land-bound existences. We were free!

CHAPTER 9

Release

In mid-April of 1957, my mother showed up at the Danbury federal prison with my two-year-old sister, Caroline. My father was happy to see his daughter, but things did not go so well with my mother. After they left, he wrote her a long letter about prison life and the "mental hell" of being "a caged animal" surrounded by criminals.

> *I'm sorry, my sweet, for this long drawn-out rather corny statement but . . . today I felt dreadfully unhappy. I looked forward to [your] visit so much! . . . I got ready hours before, couldn't sleep the night before, almost got in trouble bothering all the guards trying to find out if you were there yet!! And I find you just the same. You seem to take it quite in your stride, almost happy to be alone and do what you want—still the same quickness to react nastily at the slightest provocation, not the smallest real interest in what I think and . . . after ½ hour you were dying to go.*
>
> *Darling, I don't want pity or duty . . . I want somebody who still loves and respects me. I don't want to be pushed into any arguments about the past or the future. When I come out there will be plenty of time to discuss*

*why, how, what, etc., etc. Now my only worry must be to come out as quickly and as well as possible . . . with [your] help or without. I'd rather make up my mind now not to have any more visits until the end than have the kinds we've been having. You don't have to "stick by me" because it's the thing a wife is supposed to do but because, after due and long reflection, afterwards you'll still want me as your husband. This is **not** the difficult period—it will be after my release—and I'll then take your temper less than usual.*

But I still love and miss you horribly much.

My mother had good reason to think things over, but she didn't have a lot of time to do so. She was several months pregnant, out of work, looking for a role on stage, and behind on the apartment rent. Every morning, she spent an hour at her dressing table adjusting her makeup, curling her hair, composing her outfit. Donning her sunglasses (so as not to be recognized) and a raincoat, she slogged to auditions in drafty dark theaters on the West Side. As the weeks went by, the situation grew more dire. Her friends were worried about her; she was depressed, one confided to a columnist who wrote that she was on the verge of a breakdown. In the end, she realized she would need to sublet their apartment and move in with her mother-in-law, who already had a boarder. She was not happy about losing her independence. She resented my father's treachery, but she still loved him. And there was me to contend with, bobbing in her storm-tossed womb, my fate and my name still to be determined. Would I be Victor or Victoria?

As it was, my mother decided not only to keep my father but to try to free him. She repeatedly took the subway to Chambers Street and badgered the clerk to let her into the judge's office. Finally admitted one day late that spring, my mother pled my father's case, saying he was a true patriot, a young veteran who had simply been "misled" and made some business "mistakes" (for a long time she truly believed that). She assured the judge she had already secured a job for my father (at a car dealership) through a friend. The earlier he was released, the better his chances of getting his life back on track.

Perhaps it was small-town justice writ large. Certainly my parents existed in a privileged enclave where such things, in those days, happened. Not long after her visit, the court reduced my father's sentence, ordering for him to be released on probation on July 19, three days before my mother was due to give birth.

Upstate, in the middle of the New England woods, surrounded by eighteen-foot fences, the good news cheered my father. Prison life, he wrote to his wife, was doing him some good. It had been months since he'd had a drink. He was working out and losing weight. He was reading a lot (Nevil Shute) and taking classes in sales management. When he was free, he promised to get a job and pay the rent on the apartment. Everything would work out.

We've had rain and fog since Sunday. It felt like autumn. It's the sort of weather I love in a place like Peekskill, with a good fire going in the fireplace or walking along the river in Paris, the chestnut trees have a peculiar earthy smell after the rain which is wonderful—makes you feel healthy and glad to be alive. While I'm writing the sun is coming out.

For a moment, some of the deep cynicism he acquired during World War II vanished. There was a glimmer of hope, a kind of reborn innocence and an unfamiliar—to me, reading his letters decades later—boyish appreciation of nature and the world around him.

On the afternoon of July 25, 1957, a few days after his release from prison, my parents decided to see a movie. They stepped out of my grandmother's apartment on 97th street and crossed to the park side of Fifth Avenue and began to walk slowly downtown. My mother was wearing a yellow maternity dress, she wrote to me in a note three years before she died of Alzheimer's.

*I was walking under the trees on your father's arm. He was skinny as a rail and . . . so handsome he looked like Cary Grant. I was incredibly happy; I had succeeded in getting your father's sentence reduced. . . . I had landed a starring role in a Broadway play [*Nature's Way, *by Herman Wouk, the author of* The Caine Mutiny*] to start soon after you were born. Your father and I were in love, at least I certainly loved him and I was totally (and naïvely) optimistic about our future.*

Thank God I had no inkling of what was to come.

In the middle of the movie they had gone to see, my mother went into labor, and a few hours later, I was born.

CHAPTER 10

Days and Nights

Tuesday 4/5
N 22.12.51, W 59.42.21

In the early morning hours of our third day at sea, there was another incident.

"Woke up in my cabin after last watch . . . commotion on deck. Raining hard," I wrote in my journal.

The wind was blowing. The boat shuddered violently and heeled heavily to one side. I heard the captain yelling at Nikos on deck. I looked out my porthole and saw a gray stormy sky, cresting waves breaking in every direction. I thought we were caught in a gale and were in for a hard day at sea.

I tried to go back to sleep but I had to get up. At 6:15 I put on my rain gear, bibs, and boots. By the time I was on deck, though, the squall had passed. Nikos, who, I was learning, never complained, gave me a look that said everything—he had taken a beating, not just from the weather but also from the captain.

The first twenty-four hours at sea set a pattern. The nights were often anxious and dramatic; the days, some windy and others hot and torpid, were more instructive. At least we saw what we were doing and where we were heading. It helped to have gotten some sleep. I was not hallucinating and imagining my crewmates as murderers.

In daylight, Nikos looked less sinister. He was not a drug trafficker, it turned out, but a mild-mannered engineer. His silences were not brooding and misanthropic but a manifestation of his shyness and patience. He told me in rough English he had come to sailing late in life through his daughter, who chose it as a summer sport. Nikos would pick her up in the afternoon and find himself standing on the dock staring at the boats and the sea.

He routinely asked to be woken twenty minutes before his watch began so he could be on deck on time. Nikos did things by the book. Under duress, he was methodical and obedient; he never lost his calm demeanor.

The captain, on the other hand, was erratic. Much as I wanted to like him, I continued to feel uneasy. At times kind and inquisitive, his mood usually worsened as the day wore on into late afternoon when he would disappear into his cabin. At night, if he was not on watch, he did not want to be disturbed. On the second night, there had been another shit show, this time during Yves and Nikos's watch.

Middle of the night another commotion. Autopilot not working. Captain goes on deck. Yelling and confusion. I'm below. Leave them to it. Manage to sleep again.

The problem at night was the hand-off of the helm. It's an awkward transition from arriving on deck half-asleep to managing the movement of a fifteen-ton vessel with over one thousand square feet of sail area, being blown and tossed about at night in a cauldron of crisscrossing waves. Without landmarks, the stars, if visible, become your most reliable guideposts. In a world of movement, they stand relatively still, the mast swinging between them, orienting your inner compass; they tell you where you are. Yves and I were glued to them. We hated when the constellations we were tracking disappeared behind a veil of clouds because then we had to rely entirely on the instrument coordinates: compass heading and angle to the wind the captain had given us.

Nikos was the opposite. He never looked at the stars or felt the wind; he hardly seemed to notice the direction of the waves. He hunched over the wheel, peering at the navigation instruments, which were a second or two behind the reality of where the bow was pointing. It forced him to play a game of constant catchup that drove Yves to distraction on their joint watches. Nikos, who was hard of hearing, wouldn't take any advice about his method of navigating, and Yves came to dread handing over the helm to him. (About every half hour there'd be a switch-off.) Nikos tried to instantly align the boat direction with the instrument coordinates we had been given, sometimes hours before, regardless of the state of the wind and the waves and which way the boat was swinging at that moment. The result was either an inadvertent jibe or a broach (when the boat pulls into the wind) so violent the boat would tack in another direction on its own. The bow would dip and swoon, the sails shudder and slap loudly in the wind, the lines snapping like whiplashes. A bad hit by a large wave at such a moment could threaten to capsize the boat. The captain inevitably rushed on deck, infuriated.

We would not have had these midnight dramas if Dimitri,

like most skippers, had simply put the autopilot on until morning. Under most conditions, it was an easy, practical solution; the watch being reduced to being a lookout for errant ships or thunderstorms on the horizon. Dimitri said he was concerned the autopilot drew inordinately from the boat's battery power. He also insisted—and we mutely agreed—being at the helm and not relying on the autopilot kept us alert. It also deepened our understanding of what it means to pilot a boat, to be in control, and to step skillfully to the edge of the uncontrollable. It made us better sailors.

With GPS, digital charts, and waypoints, almost anybody today can direct a boat in a straight line to a destination a few miles away. But the same person is lost if put in a situation where there is no straight line (when you are tacking upwind), where winds and currents shift, where storms stretch over hundreds of miles, where engines are useless and batteries fail. Dimitri was trying to make us as self-reliant as he himself had become.

• • •

On the morning of that third day, I stood on deck watching the squall disappear on the horizon behind us. I was vastly relieved it hadn't been me on deck fucking up. The rain had stopped, the sea had settled, and a thin humid mist rose from the surface. I wouldn't be needing my storm jacket after all.

"Nice break," I said to the captain.

For the first time since leaving St. Martin the trade winds faltered. Dimitri reluctantly turned on the engine and I took the helm.

"Let me know when the wind comes back up," the captain said and went below.

The sun rose higher, the air grew warmer, and the last storm clouds broke up. In front of us a rainbow formed a tremendous arch, as tall and strong as the legs of the Eiffel Tower. Then it mysteriously dissipated into tinted drizzle as we passed beneath it.

I looked eastward for dark patches of wind-brushed water. For an hour we inched forward, a ruffled sea surface appearing here and there before the air boldly drew nearer. Then the wind was again upon us. The sails filled, the mast creaked, and the boat heeled slightly. We were underway again. Yves came up to relieve me at the helm, and I went below to have breakfast and write in my journal.

> *Clear skies with small white clouds. 15–17 knot winds. Perfect! I can finally walk around down below without slamming into walls. Everyone feeling better. I eat an orange and crackers. I shave, shower, and do some laundry.*

By midday, though, the wind slackened again. With the sun directly overhead, it had become oppressively hot. Yves stumbled down to his berth. An hour later, he barely roused himself for lunch. After eating a half plate of food, he went straight back down to his cabin. Something was wrong, but I didn't have time to think about it. After cleaning up the lunch dishes, it was my turn to be at the helm again.

The captain gives me close instruction on helmsmanship in light wind, micromanaging the movement of my hands on the wheel, the angle of the wind, and the destination bearing. The boat heads to starboard and before it's too late, I tilt the wheel to port, just enough before reversing course. Back and forth, back and forth. Inevitably, the boat swings too far to one side before I correct her. Instantly the sails shake angrily until I thrust the wheel hard and lean into it. Then the bow yields as she comes back into the wind. The sails bellow and snap tight again. It's taxing to do for one to two hours at a time. The sun is hot, and everyone is looking for a shred of shade.

After a while the captain saw I was managing and went below. It was a relief not to be watched over. Good to be on deck, at the helm, alone. Below, everyone seemed to be resting or asleep. I, too, began to feel relaxed, falling into the rhythm of the bow's swing. Flying fish scattered over the bow wake, leaving dark trails as they skimmed the oily surface of the water and dropped back in. I was on the verge of giving in to being hypnotized by the ocean, lulled into thinking this was the best place I could possibly be.

But I couldn't let go. I couldn't relax because of an annoying, eerie sound. Blurry voices spoke in foreign languages and garlands of music—mazurka, Chopin preludes, Beyoncé—came and went between high-pitched, whining squeaks. I thought I was hearing things. I waited. The afternoon sky turned whiter and hazy. The recurring squeal persisted. Finally, I put the boat on autopilot and glanced below. The captain was hunched over the chart table, dialing slowly, diligently, through the frequency bands of a shortwave radio. I went back to the helm, waiting for Dimitri to find the station he was looking for. But the cyclical noise went on and on. It was irritating, then maddening, as the broadcast blared indefinitely.

> *He listens for hours, at full volume, nonstop. I'm alone on deck working hard to keep the boat from heading or jiving. The main boom clatters. The wind is dying and the sea turning into a hot, still soup. The captain seems oblivious.*

Toward the end of the afternoon, I saw Yves below, finally waking up, getting something to drink and eat. I waved at him urgently to come up on deck.

"What? What is it?" He looked tired and annoyed.

"Dimitri's been listening to that noise for two hours."

"Maybe it's important. He has to talk to someone."

"He hasn't talked to anyone. It's weird."

I wanted to continue the conversation but when Yves sat down and tried to shackle to the lifeline, I noticed something was off. His hands were shaking. His face was pale.

"Are you okay?"

"I'm having one of those sun episodes. I felt it this morning at the helm. My face and neck got all hot. My legs felt weak."

What Yves called an "episode" was a form of heatstroke. I had seen this before playing tennis. Yves, usually electric on the court, racing from side to side to return everything I hit, would become lethargic and disoriented, not trying to get to a ball, missing shots wildly. If the sun got too hot, he would just resign, walking wearily off the court. It was frightening to watch, like seeing a lost dog or an animal hit by a car.

Yves said he could take the helm, but I had my doubts. He had a hard time getting positioned behind the wheel, strapping in, getting his bearings. I saw the effort in his face. The boat started to lose wind and swing.

"Right! Right! Right!" I directed him.

But Yves just moved very slowly and turned the wheel in the wrong direction. My heart sank. Suddenly I was afraid again. My friend, who was in his late sixties, might be having a serious stroke. The captain was in his cabin, bleary-eyed (I suspected he might be on meds), glued to the kind of short-wave radio last used by ships in the 1980s.

The good mood of earlier that day evaporated. In a few hours it would be dark again. The sail of the only boat we had spotted so far had disappeared below the horizon. We were now hundreds of miles away from St. Martin. Too remote to get help and perhaps, I thought, too far along to turn back.

• • •

That night we ate our dinner of pasta and broccoli quickly and in silence. Yves went straight back to bed. I was left to wash the dishes again with a long night on deck awaiting me. When I came up from the galley, there were long, slow swells, a light breeze, and stars overhead. The captain turned the helm over to me.

"She is steering herself. You barely need to correct," he told me.

He waited a few minutes to see if I was good, then he went below, leaving me alone on deck. He was doing this more. It was encouraging. It meant he had confidence in my abilities behind the wheel. But it also meant more work for me, since we didn't rotate every half hour like I did on other watches with Nikos and Yves. Dimitri would pop his head up the companionway every once in a while to make sure everything was okay but other than that, I was solo for most of the next three hours.

The evening before, Dimitri and I had talked during our watch. He had arrived on deck flashing his phone at the night sky. He had a phone app that identified the constellations. He pointed out a few I wasn't familiar with, like the Southern Cross and Centaurus. We talked about sailing. For him it had been a calling from an early age. He was racing regattas as a boy and coached sailing as a teenager. He continued to team race, circumnavigating the globe, before becoming a captain of his own charter company. But the business was just an excuse to continue living at sea. Even in his forties, he confessed to me, he couldn't imagine settling down on land. There was a spiritual component to his love of sailing, "because you are always in the presence of something bigger than you," he told me.

The conversation stalled. There was not much else in life, besides sailing, that we had in common, but we were being friendlier, which encouraged me to confess my worst fears. I sat down on the bench near the helm and looked him in the eye.

"I know we are going to hit some heavy seas soon. You have warned us that we might see thirty- or forty-knot winds and twenty-foot seas. But neither Yves, Nikos, nor I have the experience to handle this boat in a bad gale. All it takes is one mistake in a big wave for the boat to get broadsided or capsize. Will you promise me that you will stay on deck at night, all night, if we get into heavy weather?"

"No." He looked at me. I waited for a smile, for any hint of a concession, but it didn't come. "You will learn a lot in the next week. You will be able to handle it."

• • •

The next night, alone behind the helm, the seas and breeze consistent, the moon appeared in and out of the clouds. I had time to think about the day, time to take stock. The squall at dawn, the calm and cheerful morning, the hot afternoon with the bizarre radio interlude. Yves not feeling well. It was worrisome, I told myself, but not cause for panic. The shortwave obsession could be explained. Yves was ill but would likely soon recover. Perhaps even the fair weather would last too.

When later that night a massive thunderhead grew and bore down on the boat, I was again alone on deck. This time I stayed calm. I studied the cloud as it spread its cold air over us, reading its mood. I gauged the agitation of the wind and waves. I threaded the mast between its darkest folds, bracing for a bolt of lightning, a downpour, thunder. But as we passed beneath it, the cloud, like a sleeping giant, stayed mute and undisturbed.

Behind it, the clear night sky expanded and a few of the brightest stars reflected on the sea. Perhaps Dimitri was right. We would learn to handle what the ocean threw at us.

We sailed easily through the rest of that night, our first without incident. The next day, a morning glow slit open the bottom edge of the sky. Clouds slid by like transparent silk pillows. Yves showed up on deck smiling, feeling better. I pointed to a rosy smudge of white just above the horizon. Our companion sailboat had reappeared. We were not alone.

CHAPTER 11

Stuffed Animals and the Sea

In my childhood the only boats I knew were imaginary ones.

In the winter of 1961–62, when I was four and a half, we moved into a modest apartment building on East 85th Street between Park and Lexington Avenues. It was a busy, noisy cross street with a music school and a fire station down the block. The white brick building had a faded, sagging awning. There were rows of dented brass mailboxes in the entranceway and a dim, narrow lobby with one or two chairs and fake potted plants opposite the elevator. We stepped in and looked through the small round window as it rose and clunked from floor to floor.

Our apartment was one of two on the sixth floor; ours was on the left and faced the back of the building. There was a long, windowless hallway past my bedroom and my sister's bedroom, ending with my parents' bedroom—all on the right—and the living room straight ahead. Just before the living room was a short corridor on the left leading to the kitchen and a tiny guest bath and bedroom, where the stray unmarried women who looked after us stayed when my parents could afford childcare.

The only rooms with daylight were my parents' bedroom and the living room, which overlooked the roof of the low garage building on 82nd Street.

In the living room there was a yellow couch, a zebra rug, a walnut-and-black-marble bureau and a Zenith television. My mother added touches of elegance, like floor-length drapes. She placed a delicate silver cow milk dispenser on the fireplace mantlepiece and silver ashtrays and the cigarette case on the coffee table. Neither of my parents smoked, but they knew lots of people who did, and in the beginning, they threw loud, crowded parties. They liked popular jazz and samba—Dave Brubeck, Carlos Jobim, Etta James, Louis Armstrong, and Frank Sinatra. The guests—mostly actors, writers, and restauranteurs—were heavy drinkers. The cigarettes overflowed the ashtrays. They all danced, weaving their hips, their hands up in the air, until after midnight.

My room was the farthest away from the action and daylight. My window looked out on a sooty air shaft where pigeons gathered, fluttering and cooing. It had a connecting bathroom to my sister's bedroom.

My father's life, post-prison, soon returned to what it had been before. His unpredictable disappearances went on for weeks or months. His relationship with my mother was passionate and volatile. They continued to go out on the town to party—and get toasted.

A year after his release, he and my mother were coming home late, after midnight, the streets deserted, when they were pulled over by the police. My father had driven through a red light, maybe more than one. He politely answered the officers' questions and complied when they asked him to step out of the car and put him in handcuffs. My mother was not calm. She raised her voice when the police told her they were taking her husband down to the local precinct and were going to arrest and jail him for the night. She got out of the car in her bare feet and told the police they could not do that. She did not know how to drive and her children were home with a babysitter. They *had* to get home or the babysitter would leave us alone in the apartment. She followed the officers to the police car where they had put my father, calling them names. Then she hit one or two of them. When they tried to arrest her, she fled into the middle of the street. That's when a reporter took a picture of her, in her bare feet and a polka-dotted dress, the police closing in. They both spent the night in jail.

I don't remember many of my feelings as a child. I worried about my mother and I missed my father when he was away. No matter how long he had been gone or what events he missed, we ran into his arms when he walked in the door in his safari boots a day before Thanksgiving or Christmas. Sometimes he had gifts, other times all he had to offer was a bear hug and a funny face. We were happy to see him. It was so easy to be held in his strong and warm embrace that you forgave him for abandoning you. Still, we learned to be cautious too. We sensed wherever he had been was still there lurking in the background. Something was missing or had gone wrong or needed to be fixed. He would soon have to go back.

The uncertainty of his presence and my mother's moodiness took their toll.

One morning there was a loud knocking at the front door. Still in our pajamas, my father told us to answer and tell the people at the door that he was not home. While he scurried out the back door in the kitchen, I stood in front of the officers in their uniforms with their radios, their guns and clubs and let my sister do the talking. I thought of the squad car parked outside, with its light twirling. I imagined my father emerging from the basement steps and walking quickly down the street.

I had to swallow my pride when my school sent me home after Thanksgiving break because the tuition was not paid. I felt humiliated standing in the hallway outside the elevator looking at the bright yellow US Marshal eviction notice on the front door of the apartment. I knew our neighbors must have seen it. Slowly, imperceptibly, the grim anticipation of another crisis or "a scene" gripped my intestines, tightening like a wrench. I began to be careful; one moment I'd watch my step, the next I acted out angrily. Occasionally I had temper tantrums and introspective lulls, but I wasn't noticeably different from other children.

My sister and I listened to Beatles' 45s on our small square red-and-white record player: "I Want to Hold Your Hand," "Twist and Shout," "Paperback Writer," "Love Me Do." When we danced, we tried to outdo them, our parents, at who they were.

In the evenings we took baths and got into our pajamas.

We sat at the coffee table in the living room with our supper—hot dogs, sandwiches and soup, Stouffer's Welsh Rarebit, and so on—and watched 1960s television. Reruns of the *Adventures of Superman, Flipper, Mister Ed, I Dream of Jeannie*. Fantasy shows. We clapped our hands and laughed, we rolled on the rug and sang the theme songs. We groaned and changed the channel when *Father Knows Best* filled the screen. *Come on!*

When my father was home, he and I would sing the theme song to *Rawhide*: that same word, *rawhide*, repeated for two or three minutes. If he was home that time in the evening, it was because there was not enough cash for a babysitter and my mother—working six nights a week on stage—had put her foot down. *Someone* had to watch the kids. She kissed us goodnight and left before we finished our dinner.

Later, after we were in bed and the lights were out, my father would stick his head in my bedroom door.

"I'm going to get the paper at the corner," he'd say. "I'll be right back." I'd picture him walking to the newspaper stand on 86th Street and Lexington Avenue.

"Okay," I'd answer, knowing he was lying.

I felt alone at the end of the hallway, closest to the door, to the outside world. I lay there listening to the pigeons, then the fire engines and the police sirens wailing down the street. I'd imagine the vast world of the city in the night. I wondered who controlled it all. The subways rumbling beneath, the lights changing in sequence all the way down the avenue, the pipes bringing water to our faucets. There was order, and there was disorder and the lurid mayhem I'd seen on the front page of the daily newspapers. A gangster splayed on the sidewalk, jacket open, a pool of blood leaking under his head; people jumping from burning tenements; a grandmother stabbed in her bed by a burglar. Our front door had three locks on it. We were warned never to let *anyone* in.

After my father left, my sister tiptoed through the bathroom and came to my bed and whispered directions to me. Put the lamp under the small play table and place a blanket over the table. Lay the two play chairs on their sides and bolster this perimeter with large stuffed animals. This was our "boat" and the rest of the dark room was the sea. It stretched down the hallway to our parents' empty bedroom and outside the window, to our schools, through the park, all the way up to the stars. While my mother was on stage on Broadway performing in front of hundreds of people and my father was playing poker in a room above a bar, we were on our ship in the middle of the ocean.

There was always a storm and my sister always fell overboard. She called out for me to save her. I would throw her a pillow life preserver, or I would jump into the sea myself and drag her back to the boat where we would retreat under the table covered by the blanket. I would dry her off, and then we would curl up together in the quilt, under the table with the rosy light on, and sleep.

CHAPTER 12

Five Hundred Miles

Wednesday 4/6
N 23.59, W 58.25
506 miles from St. Martin
Approx 2,000 miles to Azores

The wind finally died completely, leaving first me and then Yves rattled as the boat stalled, the boom banging from side to side, the sails slapping impatiently like a matador's cape. The sun was high in the sky. We were hot and despondent after struggling for hours to direct the boat in a dying wind. When we saw the captain come up on deck, we were afraid.

The one thing Dimitri did not want to do was turn on the engine and waste valuable fuel that might be needed later. We expected him to tell us to trim the sails again or find fault with our heading. Instead, he smiled, his eyes bright as cut sapphires. "Let's go for a swim!" he said.

We were more than five hundred miles from any shore, wearing our life vests packed with AIS beacons and shackled to the safety line. Dimitri had trained us to think falling off the boat was potentially fatal. Yet we'd been staring hungrily at the cool, transparent blue water slipping by us hour by hour.

We looked at him suspiciously.

"It's my birthday!" he added.

We threw off our gear and went below for our bathing suits. Dimitri was the first to leap from the deck into the flat still water, followed quickly by Yves. They began to swim away from the boat. Then I jumped in. I started to follow them but stopped after not more than ten or fifteen yards. I turned around, looking at *Orion*, the silky deep blue water all around us, the white sky. It wasn't real—the unbelievable distance that separated us from the rest of the world, as if we were on a set of a film with cutouts of the ship and the sea. If you drew back up into the sky, like a camera on a drone, we would become these tiny dots, attached by gravity and fear to the mothership. The water, blank and inhuman, stretching to the horizon on every side.

I dipped my head beneath the surface to see the dark outline of the hull and the short keel underwater. It looked so small and insignificant, like a piece of driftwood in outer space. When I resurfaced, Nikos had jumped into the water too. There was no one left on board the boat. It was insane, like sailors in the eighteenth century suffering from calenture, we had all leaped thoughtlessly into the ocean.

I didn't think the boat was drifting, but I did a quick few strokes until my hand reached the ladder on the transom. Then I held on, waiting for the others.

After lunch, the captain turned the shortwave radio on again. The noise droned on for an hour before we heard him speak.

"Whiskey, five-eight, two-five. November two-three five-nine."

Dimitri repeated the boat's coordinates and waited. Amid the static, a faint voice responded practically inaudible, as if on the other side of the earth.

"Roger!"

After a short discussion, sometimes in Greek, sometimes in English, Dimitri would thank whoever it was he was speaking to and begin the search for another voice. When he was done talking, he turned off the radio and came back on deck.

"We're on the edge of the high. If we go further east, we will lose the wind. We must head north, to 30 degrees, not much more," he told us.

"Is this how you get your weather reports?" I asked.

"Yes."

"It takes a long time."

"I must find the right frequency. One minute you cannot hear and then it is clear as a bell. It depends, too, on the weather where we and they are. Sometimes it is hard to find a signal."

"Who are you talking to?"

"Friends of mine. Captains of big ships. One is in Madagascar. Another is going through the Panama Canal . . . On shortwave radio you can reach anyone. Even in the China Sea."

Dimitri moved to the stern of the boat and pointed to a wire taped to the steel bimini frame.

"This is the antenna" he said. "It's old-fashioned, but it's free!"

The good news was, I guess, that the captain was paying attention to the weather. The bad news was that he had to spend hours weeding through shortwave frequencies to find his friends, and even then he wasn't accessing anything like accurate, timely information about weather fronts near our location. He certainly was not receiving customized satellite updates and forecasts. Later I wrote in my journal:

Problem is in a couple of days we will be sailing north of the 30th parallel waiting for news on which low-pressure system is going to carry us to the Azores if it doesn't pummel us first. And our captain is going to be dependent on his antiquated weather reporting system for the rough location, track, duration and strength of a storm. Because that is what a low-pressure system usually is in the middle of the ocean: a fucking storm.

It turned out Dimitri didn't really care. That afternoon, after our swim in the ocean, he argued that his shortwave radio was as good a way as any other to get weather reports because, it turns out, he didn't trust weather forecasts in the first place, given by *anybody*.

"How can they know what is happening here?" He pointed to the deck of the boat and then the sky. "We are in the ocean. There are no instruments here. We are here. We are the only people who know what is happening here right now!"

• • •

That night Dimitri made a celebratory curry dinner. We had sailed over five hundred miles, and it was his birthday. For the first time on the trip we drank alcohol, splitting a beer between two people. There was conversation, I don't remember what it was about, but Dimitri, usually in a hurry to get back to his cabin, allowed it to go on. After dinner he poured us a little wine. He wanted to dwell in the camaraderie. He had spoken via the satellite phone with his girlfriend earlier—after all, it was his birthday. I'd seen her pictures on Instagram: a young, attractive illustrator, the artist who had made the paintings on the boat. On Instagram he posted selfies of them holding hands and leaping in the air on a Caribbean beach. From what he told us, it seemed she was the more practical one. She kept him tethered to the realities of running a charter business. She encouraged him to post updates on social media and plan theme-based charter weekends, but he had little interest in growing his charter business, in acquiring a fleet of spacious, popular catamarans and making money. His ambition was to enter the reestablished Golden Globe solo race around the world without the help of modern technology. "*That* I want to do," he told us.

Later, after dinner, Yves and I kicked back on deck and listened to music and sang. Yves, who for years played saxophone with a touring band, knows classic jazz—who played what instrument on which track on an album cut in 1958. He also has a knack for singing American standards. He can put on the voice of any crooner: Bing Crosby, Nat King Cole, Frank Sinatra. That night, among the songs he sang was Chet Baker's "My Funny Valentine." Yves knew all the words, and I hummed along, joining with the refrain and the lines I sort of remembered. It was a relief that evening, under the stars, to put some of my anxieties on the back burner. As challenging and frightening as the ocean can be, it's also healing.

In New York, before I left, I'd made doctors' appointments. I worried about getting a kidney stone or suffering a bout of diverticulitis on board the boat. In the weeks before we left for St. Martin, my lower back tightened so painfully I tried to get a steroid spinal shot. I nagged doctors for prescriptions against bacterial infections and, especially, tranquilizers for my insomnia. I packed beta-blockers for my heart palpitations and panic attacks. I imagined every bad thing that could possibly happen to me would happen.

But on board *Orion*, despite being bruised by run-ins with sharp corners, despite my hands cramping from pulling on sail lines, despite the beating we took from the elements five days into the trip, physically *I was just fine*. My back didn't hurt at all. I had no ailments. No headaches, no palpitations. At night, surprisingly, I dropped effortlessly into a blissful hour or two of deep, blackout sleep between watches.

That night the two of us Francophones sang anthems of American soulfulness and optimism. Even if everything wasn't okay back home in America, we hoped for the best. We existed in the present. We were alive! The weather was good! We had escaped the clickbait headlines, the nonstop scrolling, the ingestion of information about antibodies and vaccines, bombings and polls and food prices and war. Out on the sea, rolling with the waves, we found a paradigm of freedom. We sang because we wanted to. We sang because this was what men did at sea to keep the demons at bay. Our voices trailed out underneath the tilting constellations, barely existent, melodies catching unknown frequencies to travel on through the night.

CHAPTER 13

Cotopaxi

Music, like the sea, carries us along. It colors our days. It reminds us nostalgically of where we have been. It slings hope, like a lariat, around the unknown future.

The soundtrack to my parents' marriage came to a peak in the market town of Otavalo, high up in the Andes of Ecuador. On a clear June day in 1963, the snow-capped peak of Cotopaxi visible above them, they drove across the Andean plateau in my father's light-blue Chevrolet pickup truck to one of the Spanish colonial churches in Otavalo and finally got married. Legal and under God.

I know this, in part, because my younger half sister, Claudie, gave me my parents' wedding rings in a box after my father died in 2011. The rings are inscribed "Guy-Betsy 6-15 54-63," the date when they purportedly got married and the years they had been together. The rings were still shiny, the edges sharp. They'd never been put on any fingers.

A few years before, in late December of 1960, my mother's mother died of cancer in Germany where she had moved to be reunited with my grandfather, the count. My mother, acting in a play at the time, could not attend the funeral. But that summer, she went with Guy to meet her father in Switzerland to discuss my grandmother's estate, a remnant of which was left to cover my sister's and my education. Two years later, when we were living in the dark apartment on 85th Street, my father walked in from a trip to Europe and announced his ship had come in.

He bought my mother a fur coat. He told her to quit her job on Broadway where she was playing a small part in a long-running hit to pay the bills. She hesitated. She had heard these promises before. But this time there was money in the bank. My father had secured a large amount of cash on the signing of a contract, he said. Moreover, they were *guaranteed* monthly income for years to come.

My mother went along. She quit the play. We took a family vacation to Jamaica.

At the time, my father was traveling frequently to South America. He told my mother he had invested in a gold mine in the Amazon jungle of Ecuador. He showed her pictures of a large pinkish white stucco house surrounded by palm trees and gardens, a former embassy he was thinking of renting in Quito. Why not get out of town for a while and move to Ecuador? She could paint and indulge in her new passion for photography. There would be a big garden for the children and a menagerie of possible pets—dogs, rabbits, monkeys, parrots, horses, anything she wanted.

In June of 1963, she went with Guy to Ecuador to visit and fell in love with the Andean landscape, the colonial architecture, the indigenous markets. The house on the Avenida de Colon was grand, a dream come true. They arranged for us to attend an international school in Quito. Before they left, they drove across to Otavalo and married. My father didn't have the rings; they were still being engraved, he promised. A few months later, he gave her a half-moon chunk of gold from his mine that she wore around her neck, and he put the other half on his key chain.

In August, my parents sublet the apartment in New York, and we moved into the white house in Quito and enrolled in school there. For a six-year-old, it was intoxicating to see long-horned oxen pulling wagons of hay in the street, seeing magenta and midnight-blue-clothed women with gold earrings in their nose nursing their child in the open-air marketplace, the baskets heaped with vegetables, the sides of cow hanging on hooks covered in flies, a courtyard bullfight (without swords) at a remote hacienda on a dusty Sunday afternoon, the air smelling of burning eucalyptus leaves, and the volcanoes in the distance. It was a magical world, the most enduring experience of my childhood, even if it did not last long.

On November 23, 1963, all the church bells in Quito tolled, mourning President John F. Kennedy's assassination. But the residual goodwill for Americans in Latin America was fast evaporating. The political mood had changed since the Cuban revolution. The welcome mat was wearing thin and, at the mine, extracting gold from the dense jungle earth was more difficult and costly than expected.

By the spring of 1964, my father was often away again, either in the jungle or in Europe trying to raise more funds. He and my mother drifted apart. Betsy confided to her friend Luce de Peron, the wife of the great South American painter Oswaldo Guayasamin (his portrait of my mother with the crescent hunk of gold around her neck hangs in a museum in Quito), that she was unhappy and there were frequent fights between them. "Your father was a violent, dangerous man," Luce told me decades later when I returned to Ecuador on a writing assignment. It was my mother, though, who took a shot at my father, thinking he was a thief breaking into the house when he returned in the middle of the night, without advance notice, from a trip abroad. There were other accidents. I was hit in the head with a brick by a worker, suffered a bloody concussion, and ended up in the hospital. My sister sliced open her wrist when she put her hand through a terrace glass door.

By the following summer, the mine was running out of cash to pay the workers, maintain the machinery, and fly the planes to and from the jungle encampment. My father did not realize the thick black mucus oozing beneath his boots in the jungle was the real prize and would revolutionize the Ecuadorian economy. He kept returning to Europe, hoping to find more investors—in gold. In the end, he sold his multithousand-acre concession in the jungle for a nominal sum to a company called Texaco.

My mother saw the writing on the wall. She flew to New York on her own to talk to her agent, to scout out work opportunities. While she was in New York, she saw a production of a Chekhov play in Greenwich Village and met a Latin actor in the cast. He was not a handsome man like my father, nor was he quick and playful. He spoke slowly and methodically. He played chess and read books about philosophy. He had a floor-to-ceiling collection of classical records that they listened to in his tiny apartment with a partial view of the Hudson River. They became lovers, and a few months later we returned to New York—with the promise that we'd visit Quito, the house, and our pets—the dogs, rabbits, and a monkey named Kiki—again soon.

For a while we continued to live in the dark apartment. My father slept on a cot in the dining area and read paperback mysteries. There were no more parties, no more music. One late afternoon, after I'd come home from school, my mother answered the phone and started weeping. Our dogs in Quito were all dead, she told me; poisoned meat had been thrown over the gates. The lease on the house on Avenida de Colon was not renewed. We would not be going back to Ecuador.

When the phone company cut off our telephone service in New York, my father (who was opening a restaurant on Lexington Avenue) installed a payphone in the kitchen hallway. We heard my parents arguing, doors slamming, the sound of my father hitting my mother, of him in tears, begging her not to leave him. Those memories never leave you. They may seem to disappear, to go underground, but secretly they follow you wherever you go, like waves in the middle of the ocean.

CHAPTER 14

Spinnakers, Risotto, and Latitude

Weds 4/6–Sat 4/9
N 23.59, W 58.25–N28.44, W 53.15
965 miles from St. Martin
1,740 miles still to go

For the next few days, the captain steered us north to find more wind. At first it was agreeable. The trade winds had lessened, but we were still making well over a hundred miles a day. We learned the ropes; we mastered our tacks. When we weren't on watch there was time to read, to practice tying knots, to wash some socks and underwear. One morning Yves convinced the captain to allow him to call Pamela. They had a two-minute conversation. We talked about the two-minute conversation for an afternoon. We marked our chart. We finished and traded books. It was almost normal.

On Thursday afternoon, the wind slid down southwest, behind the boat, and Dimitri decided to put up the spinnaker, a giant fluffy and floppy sail used to speed up the boat when traveling downwind. Spinnakers are complicated to rig and delicate to handle. We had to learn new lines: top pole, bottom pole, spinnaker halyard, topping lift, and foreguy. I came up on deck midway through the lesson. Dimitri lost track of who he had told what.

His instructions were mixed up. I got annoyed again. Tired of the reprimands. Tension between the captain and me.

I didn't understand why we were wasting time learning about the spinnaker, a dangerous sail for an inexperienced crew to handle under high-wind conditions. We should've been practicing reefing and preparing for the heavy seas we would soon face. Nikos, who was by then a friend, advised me quietly, as Dimitri went on a tirade, to just keep silent and listen. "It is the best thing to do," he said.

As it was, the wind was too shifty and died; the spinnaker was dropped. It was a relief for all of us, who were getting tired and thirsty. The captain turned on the engine *and* the autopilot. We caught up on sleep and took naps.

The next afternoon, when we were being pushed downwind by a moderate breeze, Yves mentioned the spinnaker again. I gave him a dirty look, but he just laughed. He had not tired of playing up to the captain in his quest to be top seadog and first mate. Sure enough, a few minutes later, the captain ordered us to haul the spinnaker out of its sack. It was easier this time to raise and set the sail, but the wind was weak and again it kept shifting, which made keeping the sail full a tricky and tiring proposition.

During the exercise Yves kept trying to make light of the situation, heave-oohing, singing chanties and barking orders at me and Nikos, when he wasn't running up to the bow to help the captain. He was for all intents and purposes acting as first mate. I didn't let all this get to me, but neither did I join in Yves's folksy cheerleading.

It didn't matter. While I was at the helm, the spinnaker caught on the bowsprit and ripped slightly.

"I'm sorry," I said to the captain.

"It's not your fault!" Dimitri insisted.

He offered to take the helm, which I happily relinquished, but he fared no better at the wheel. The spinnaker kept catching on the bow, ripping until the bottom edge was almost torn clear of the rest of the sail. It was becoming an expensive mistake. Yves ran up to the bow and tried futilely to hold the foot of the sail together with clothespins. I, too, dashed up repeatedly—neither of us clipped to the safety line—to clear the flapping spinnaker from the point of the bowsprit.

In the end, though, the sail had to be taken down again. We rinsed the fabric along the tear with fresh water, dried it in the sun, and held it together as the captain, like a surgeon, meticulously tape-stitched it back together, a task that took hours.

While we were mending the spinnaker, Yves would excuse himself to run down to the stove and check on his rising dough. I'm not sure how it happened, but on the same day I was scheduled to cook dinner—a mushroom risotto (made with packets of dried portobello mushrooms I had brought with me)—Yves decided to bake a loaf of homemade bread. The bread, though, was taking much longer to make than he thought, and he was still at it when I started to prep my risotto, chopping shallots and mushrooms and making a broth. Every few minutes he had to interrupt my cooking to open the oven door and rotate his half-raw, half-burnt bread. The oven burner, oddly, was neither at the top or the bottom of the oven but in the back. And since the boat was still slightly heeled, the bread kept sliding back into the flame and burning, while the other side remained uncooked.

Anyone else would've abandoned the project, but Yves kept at it. His new best friend, the captain, was concerned about the bread, too, and Nikos also was inquiring. To make matters even more annoying, every time Yves opened the oven door, we had to slide out the small butter knife that the captain had provisionally wedged against the broken top-range burner knob to keep the flame alive under my pan of simmering risotto. Too much cooking and my risotto would become soggy, too little or intermittent a flame and it might remain hard and gritty. I wanted to strangle Yves, but he finally gave up on the bread.

We sat down to dinner at the cockpit table, fair skies above us. The risotto was good, the pot scraped clean as the crew went back for more. Yves, though, remained glum throughout the meal. He'd had a bad day. First the spinnaker, which was his idea, then the inedible loaf of bread. There was the temptation to twist the knife in a bit, to relish Yves's misstep, to watch him wriggle as he would've done to me, but I couldn't do it. To witness Yves fail was too painful. Like many of my buddies, Yves covers up disappointment or weakness so thoroughly he almost convinces you he doesn't feel *anything*. But the shame goes deep, especially if it's public and, in this case, in front of the captain he was trying so hard to impress.

After dinner, Yves and I did the galley cleanup together. Once the dishes were done, there was nothing left but the plastic plate holding the scarred, half-baked loaf of bread. I didn't have the heart to throw it out.

"Let's toast it for dessert," I said.

We tore off pieces of crust and soft dough, stuck them on a fork, browned the chunks of bread over the open flame of the stove, lathered them in butter and honey and popped them into our mouths like a kind of sea doughnut. We ate one after the other until there was only the burnt crust to toss.

So it went, day by day, our small failures and triumphs as we sailed farther north, separating from the tropics one degree in latitude at a time. We had started at 19 degrees north of the equator and by Friday morning we had reached N 27. Three days later, one week from our departure, we passed N 30. The sea turned cobalt gray; the waves combed with froth. The air, chilly at the end of the day, became cold enough during our midnight watches to numb our gloved fingers.

CHAPTER 15

Faraway Shores

Sometimes, on a late Sunday summer night during my childhood in the dark apartment, my mother (after her Sunday performance, with the next day off) and my father bundled us in blankets and carried us down to his small, green sports car. They packed us in the back seat area, a leather cocoon that smelled of my father's aftershave and my mother's perfume. We jolted from the curb, my mother hissing and holding out her arm as my father raced up the avenue, running "pink" lights and dodging the few taxis still left on the streets. We crossed the park, then we left the streetlamps and neon store signs behind us as my father accelerated onto the West Side Highway and the darkness of the woods enveloped us.

We would wake momentarily when we arrived at Pinafore Farm, which was not a farm but a modest stone-and-wood house deep in the hilly Connecticut woods near Danbury. It was owned by my mother's close friend and mentor, Jeanie, a theater producer and her husband, Philip, a retired general who had fought in World War II and Korea. They were older than my parents and all-American. Jeanie kept her hair in a bun and wore an apron. She was in the kitchen cooking and baking most of the time when we visited. Philip barked out orders and made bad jokes as if he were still in uniform.

They would be in their bedroom on the second floor with their two dogs (they had no children) when we arrived, with the light on and the door open a crack. My mother would peak in to say hello and then take us up the narrow creaking stairs to the attic room where my sister and I slept.

I don't remember my father once we arrived. It was as if he went straight back to the city or disappeared into a room and never came out. Maybe it was because he really wasn't there after my parents separated. The general, too, after teasing me mercilessly, would go off in his black Thunderbird to play golf. As for my mother, she would be in her room reading a script or sunning herself on the terrace. But truthfully, I didn't miss any of the adults. They didn't matter to me.

My fascination was partially with the house itself, an oasis of calm Americana with its deep-cushioned paisley sofas, lettuce-leaf-shaped ashtrays, and ceramic hunting dogs on the big stone mantlepiece. This was the suburban America I saw on television and experienced when I was invited to my schoolmates' country homes. It was secure. It had been paid for—its permanency was palpable. There was even a cubbyhole for golf bags and, as evidence of legitimacy, black-and-white photographs on the stairs of Jeanie shaking hands with Hollywood stars and American presidents.

It was the New England landscape, the timbered hillsides outside, though, that had me down at the sun-porch glass door as soon as the sun rose, panting with the dogs to escape. Jeanie was usually the only other person up. She would give me some breakfast and hand me my fishing rod as I bounded out the door.

I ran down the slight hill to the wooden bridge that

spanned the culvert that joined the small deep pond on the right, where the black snakes lived, and the long shallow "lake" on the left that stretched into the woods. Before crossing the bridge there was a hard mud beach on the lake shore where the aluminum rowboat was kept upside down to keep the rain out. I would turn it over (I never saw anyone else use it) and push out into the lake using one oar in the stern like a gondolier. Most of the so-called lake was no more than a foot or two deep—it was really a spring-fed swamp that had been cleared of trees. I could circumnavigate the whole body of water in ten minutes, which in my imagination was a river, a bay, or the open sea. It was whatever I wanted it to be.

Standing on "the deck" of my aluminum rowboat, I explored new lands or fired off a broadside of canons to fend off a British man-of-war. I identified with rebels. I pretended I was a Mohawk scout. Most often, though, I was just a boy peering into the murky water at tadpoles or the pulsing gills of sunnies, listening to the whistle of a hawk circling way above.

I would stay outside all day.

It was a relief to get away from the adult world, the fights and hysteria. I built a secret shelter between two boulders, and I sat there protected, overseeing the lake, listening as a single-engine plane droned way above in the lonely sky.

When I was older, I ventured into the woods on the far side of the pond. I crossed the swamp and found an old logging trail that went on for miles. It was as if the farther and deeper I went into the woods, the more I found myself.

Once, years later, my mother took my sister and me up to Canada to visit an old friend of hers, a gruff Hollywood actor who had a beard, drank too much scotch, and owned a house on a remote, thirty-one-mile-long lake. There was a picture at home of him holding me on his knee when I was a toddler. I had always liked him. He was funny and kind to me. On our first day in Canada, he took me to the boathouse. Inside, tied to the dock, was a varnished wood lake boat with a small outboard engine.

"Go out whenever you want," he said to me.

I looked around with disbelief at the axed wood crossbeams of the boathouse and the water beyond, the oars and fishing rods in their racks, the cans of gas and motor oil, the canoes on the dock, the lapstrake-hull motorboat floating at my feet. I had learned about outboard motors with two friends on Long Island earlier that summer, and the next morning, before anyone else was up, I walked down to the boathouse on my own. I looked around and found a jacket hanging on the wall and a fishing rod on a rack. I got into the boat, pulled out the choke, pumped the gas line, and tugged on the pull-start cord a few times. Then I put-putted out into the lake that stretched before me for miles. It was mysterious and fulfilling to be in control, to be free to do as I liked, to imagine the dark faraway shorelines of distant islands underfoot and the blue water extending forever on the other side.

PART II
The Storm

Odysseus

Always the setting forth was the same,
Same sea, same dangers waiting for him
As though he had got nowhere but older.
Behind him on the receding shore
The identical reproaches, and somewhere
Out before him, the unraveling patience
He was wedded to. . . .

The knowledge of all that he betrayed
Grew till it was the same whether he stayed
Or went. Therefore he went. And what wonder
If sometimes he could not remember
Which was the one who wished on his departure
Perils that he could never sail through,
And which, improbable, remote, and true,
Was the one he kept sailing home to?

—W. S. Merwin

CHAPTER 16
The Weather Map

Sunday April 10
N 30.23, W 52.16
1,089 miles from St. Martin

On *Orion*, I waited for a sense of calm and relief, that feeling of unity and peacefulness I usually experienced on the water. But it never came. Whenever I felt trust and confidence, an incident would undermine it. Another shit show at night, a leak in my cabin, a strange vibration in the hull, another two-hour shortwave radio broadcast. It made me uneasy to witness the growing pile of clothes on the floor of the captain's cabin and to see the strange look on his face in the middle of the night—was it a bad dream? Was it anger or longing?

Mostly, though, my anxiety sprang from the unavoidable reality that we were heading north. I knew as we passed the thirtieth parallel and approached the Maginot Line of 35 degrees latitude, there was an increasing chance we would run into severe weather.

Last night (Sat) the captain gathered us around the navigation table to show us a "current" weather forecast map (cobbled together from his various sources). The news was not good. Three close-set low fronts were approaching us from the northwest with areas of gale force winds, and a massive low-pressure storm with developing hurricane winds was just northeast of the Azores. The Azores are still 1,600 miles away, so there is good chance that that low will move southeast, away from us, but so far it has not budged and, according to the captain, there is a chance another low will form to replace it when the first one moves off.

Unknown to us, the news of the heavy weather in midocean had reached the small fleet of yachties who were prepping and waiting in Bermuda and the Caribbean to start their own transatlantic crossings. Any planned departures were abruptly canceled as sailors gawked at the treacherous low fronts and the accompanying high winds—indicated by fletched arrows on the map—rising above thirty to forty knots. In fact, we had not seen any other vessels apart from a tanker in the past forty-eight hours. The one other sailboat we had spotted earlier—much larger than ours—had long since turned south and disappeared over the horizon.

The strategy for the moment, the captain told us as we huddled close in near darkness, would be to thread a path between the high pressure (where it is calm) to our east, which is protecting us, and the approaching lows to our northwest. Riding the front of those lows eastward, he said, we must avoid getting pinched and overtaken on all sides by lows as the high pressure dips south.

After the weather briefing, we had dinner. Little was said at the table, and Yves and I each had an espresso cup of red wine. Nikos tried to distract me. He asked me if the police in the United States enforced drinking and driving laws. How much were the tickets? Were violators sent to jail? For how long? I answered his questions impatiently.

"What did you think of the weather forecast?" I finally blurted out when the captain went below. Nikos looked at me calmly, as if I had asked him how old his children were.

"The reason I come on this trip was to learn from a man with a lot of experience how to deal with these kinds of dangerous situations," he said.

I wished I could be as calm and confident as Nikos and Yves seemed to be, but the news about the confluence of lows we faced had unnerved me. One could hardly imagine a worse weather scenario. As soon as I saw the massive low—with near-*hurricane* winds—over the Azores, I thought, "That's it, we're doomed." All the foreboding feelings I had about the trip reemerged. The cemetery, the bad omens, the missing crew. My hallucinations even returned that night, shading entire portions of the sky in a red-purple nebula. When Yves later commented nonchalantly, "Oh well, lows were bound to develop," I exploded. It was unfair and unwarranted but, as far as I was concerned, it was Yves and the captain who had put us in this situation.

I went below to get some sleep, and I had nightmares.

A few hours later, I woke up for my 3:30 a.m. watch. The wind had come up and the temperature had dropped. Something inside me had changed too. I opened my closet and fished out my heavy-weather offshore jacket. Its luminous stripes shone like orange construction cones on a highway at night. The dead certainty of rough weather and storms ahead bucked up my pride and courage. I zipped up the thickly insulated, stiff coat collar like I was locking myself in Gore-Tex armor. I repacked my inflatable life vest with its brass oxygen cylinders and AIS electronic beacon and snapped it tightly around my chest. Climbing on deck, *right on time*, dressed in my full regalia with my headlamp properly affixed, I felt unexpectedly confident and capable.

A perky northwest breeze filled the sails and the sky glistened with neon stars. The captain greeted me from the helm, and we lapsed into a comfortable silence, each looking out at a different part of the ocean. Strangely, there seemed at moments like these an understanding between us. We were both solitaries, both awed by the empty promise of the night sky, mollified by the movement of the waves. Being at sea was almost a sickness, an addiction we shared and a challenge we were eager to face. There was a look in his eyes as he mutely stared out at the water that reminded me of me.

Later, alone at the helm as the gray light of morning came up, I saw the shiny, black fluke of a whale rise briefly above a cresting wave in front of the bow and disappear.

CHAPTER 17

Good Winds and Bad

Monday, April 11
N 32.17, W. 49.19
1,305 miles from St. Martin
1,421 miles from the Azores

The next day and night, the good strong breeze from the northwest continued. In twenty-four hours we made 219 miles. The progress energized us. The captain, too, was inspired in the galley. He used up some of the last fresh vegetables on board to make a Greek salad and followed that with a bacon and zucchini pasta for dinner.

> *All in a good mood. Overnight sailing was lovely, and this morning was fun with following seas and 14 kts breeze. . . . Later, I heard Yves and the captain talking about the weather map. The captain said that at the fast clip we were moving, we could get to Horta, in the Azores, in another five or six days.*

Horta, on the quiet remote Azorean island of Faial, is legendary to sailors and yachtsmen. It's the only safe harbor to be found crossing the Atlantic from the west or the east. Grateful crews have festooned its seawalls and stone piers with colorfully painted murals representing their ships. They celebrate by getting drunk in a one-hundred-plus-year-old bar called Peter's Café Sport, a place for "people who move among the waves with life between their fists." Scrimshaw has been made and sold in an adjoining museum-cum-store since the whaling era. Yves and I had looked forward to visiting. Though Horta was not officially on our itinerary, Dimitri promised that if we had a fast crossing, we would stop there before sailing on to the capital, Ponta Delgada, on São Miguel, the largest Azorean Island. To think that we might be in Horta in less than a week seemed too good to be true.

Yves

By late on Tuesday, the seas had risen considerably. The wind blew harder, the shrouds (steel cables that stabilize the mast) vibrated like the strings of a cracked cello.

I felt we had an inordinate amount of sail up (two foresails, one rigged on a pole) for midocean eighteen-knot-conditions with an inexperienced crew, but Dimitri strategized like a racing captain. He constantly looked for ways to balance the boat and keep us moving as fast as possible. The wind kept rising, though, overpowering *Orion* as we surfed down the side of larger and steeper waves. The person at the helm had to fight the tendency of the bow to swing upwind by using all his strength to push the rudder in the opposite direction. It was exhausting work, and that evening the struggle did not end well.

Another shit show. I was at the helm for a couple of hours negotiating 10–15-foot seas with the 52-foot boat sliding from side to side as it schussed down the blue-black swells, the bow-wake exploding in an outburst of foam. Yves and Nikos were also on deck. The boat's heeling and sideways motions were getting more emphatic as the seas continued to grow and wind gusts were hitting 22, 23, and then 25, 26 knots per hour, flattening the water on top of the waves.

"The gusts over 20 knots are getting more consistent," I told Yves and Nikos. But they didn't think it was considerable enough to wake up the captain, who was down below asleep. After all, we were now experienced seadogs.

"It just hit 32!" I called out to them.

"Oh, you're just hallucinating again," Yves yelled back at me.

Meanwhile, overweight, dark rain clouds were

approaching from our port side. When the captain finally poked his head up a few minutes later, I told him we were getting gusts to 30 mph. He waved off my warning and disappeared again.

I couldn't believe it. It seemed we were about to repeat the fracas of the first night of the trip, only this time we were mid-ocean facing not a twenty-minute squall but potentially the first of several serious gales.

The last daylight was fading, and I was preparing to end my four-hour day watch when we were barraged by cold sheets of rain and knock-over gusts of wind. The captain bounded up the companionway barking orders. "Release the outhaul! Take in the main."
The problem was we still had two foresails up—one on the pole. It was getting dark and we were confused about which sails the captain was referring to and the order in which to trim the lines. Then the rain turned into a deluge. My jacket was drenched. Trickles of cold water slid up my arm sleeves, down onto my chest and legs. Meanwhile the constant stream of water pouring off my hood made it impossible to see. The captain was yelling above the sound of the wind as we tried to take down the secondary foresail and reef the main and the genoa.
"Don't just stand there," he shouted at me amid the confusion. "Get the lines cleaned up!"
"I get it!" I yelled back at him, taking a step toward him, looking him straight in the eye. "I fucking get it!"

(*What I was trying to convey was that he had screwed up by not reefing earlier and was unnecessarily taking it out on me.*) He stared back at me with a surprised look on his face. I had stepped over the line. He wouldn't forget that. But he paused to take it in, and he stopped yelling.

It wasn't until 8:30 that we put the boat on autopilot and sat down for dinner, bracing ourselves at the saloon table below deck. Dimitri passed us bowls of warmed-up canned soup, which we kept clutched in our hands so they didn't flip over into our laps. At my prodding, Yves talked to the captain. He told Dimitri I had tried to let him know about the wind so we could reef the sails *before* the heavy weather hit. (We were not allowed to alter the sail trim without the captain's say-so.) We were all tired from being at the helm in heavy seas and we needed some sleep. The captain was conciliatory. He altered the watch schedule so we would each have an extra hour of rest that night. We slurped the remainder of our soup in silence and then we went to our cabins for a nap before beginning the night watch.

In my cabin I noticed water dripping from the ceiling and down the side of the seaside wall. I'd wipe it dry with a towel, but a few minutes later it would be dripping again. At first I thought it might be coming from the ceiling hatch. Dimitri and I double-checked that the latches were locked. Still the dripping continued, dampening my clothes and sleeping bag. (The captain offered neither an apology nor explanation.) It was getting harder to find a dry corner of the mattress to lie down on.

I turned off the light and braced myself against one wall of the cabin, but I could not sleep. We were heeled heavily over to one side; the ocean waves pounded my side portal window, making it look like a washing machine. The mast shook loudly. The walls of my cabin were shimmering with rivulets of water. A wave of panic came over me. I imagined the gale rising, the wind becoming much worse than it already was. I thought this is it. We are going to go down in a storm tonight.

Strangely, my fear didn't last or seem to matter. I was too worn down to care anymore, and I kept a part of me in reserve—a separate new self that floated beside the old one, issuing gentle words of caution and calming observations. There was no reason or point in freaking out. I reminded myself there had been other moments of panic, of surety that disaster awaited, not just on *Orion* but throughout my life. If there were two possible outcomes to a situation, I inevitably picked the negative one. I regarded every promise with suspicion, a rosy outlook with skepticism. Partly it was the pessimistic, drug-consumed culture of the post–Vietnam War era. Partly because I'd learned early on that couples don't stay married forever, that not all fathers emerge triumphant from their troubles, that money and luck do run out.

On the boat that night, I reminded myself I was in capable hands. Dimitri might be erratic, but he was a formidable sailor who had experienced weather of all kinds. I recalled a few days earlier stepping on deck one morning after a rough night, the sky gray but dry. The wind and seas irritated but drained of fury. The captain was sitting at the helm, one arm casually draped along the side of the boat, with a content expression on his face, as if the sea were a recalcitrant pet he had just tamed.

After my first watch that night I managed to fall asleep, and I woke up refreshed. The seas were still high, but the wind had dropped into the high teens and soon there was light. Dimitri passed the helm to me as soon as I arrived and went down to make coffee. We passed through another double-arched rainbow. I saw a dark flash in the water, then another and another. I looked across the valley of cresting waves. There were dolphins everywhere. I called out to Dimitri and he came back on deck. We watched together as dozens of pods, hundreds and hundreds of dolphins, appeared leaping in the waves around us, surfing the bow wake. Heralding our arrival to nowhere.

CHAPTER 18

Passages

*Love, like a carefully loaded ship
Crosses the gulf between the generations . . .*
—Antoine de Saint-Exupéry

My father, too, weathered storms in the North Atlantic, not far from the waters we were sailing. He was twenty-one, going the other way, fleeing the war in Europe. On December 21, 1940, hundreds of desperate passengers, French soldiers who had escaped the Germans alongside American refugees, boarded the USS *Siboney*, a former mail ship and World War I troop carrier, in Lisbon, bound for New York.

The old ship was more than four hundred feet long and the deck looked to be at least thirty feet above the sea. My father and other young men leaned on the rail, looking at the water slide by beneath them at more than fifteen miles per hour. They kept an eye on the waves, particularly when the weather turned stormy, but they had confidence in the power and size of their ship. To the weary and excited passengers on *Siboney*, the Atlantic simply needed to be crossed; it was the final, by then, largely symbolic hurdle on their way to freedom and a new life in America.

What my father recalled was drinking and playing poker with the other French soldiers aboard the ship. They talked about their escapes from the Germans. They thought about those they had left behind. They exhorted Roosevelt to bring America into the war and defeat Hitler. Prominent among the circle of cardplayers was the celebrated French aviator and writer Antoine de Saint-Exupéry, the author of *The Little Prince*.

My father and the writer had a few things in common. They had both lived in Algiers (where my father was born), they spoke Arabic, and loved flying. Movement had meaning to them, albeit in different ways. My father wanted to manhandle space, get through it as fast as possible. Saint-Exupéry luxuriated in its poetry. He wrote stories about flying through the clouds above the Andes and landing in the Sahara Desert. To Saint-Exupéry, a pioneering pilot, empty space had a spiritual component. To my father who came of age as man's techno-mechanical ingenuity ransacked the marketplace, space was an obstacle—fast cars and, soon, jets would be a way to erase it.

Still, Saint-Exupéry's stories appealed to my father, who had read Alexandre Dumas in school and thought of himself as a nineteenth-century Romantic, an adventurer, a musketeer who drove a Bugatti. He was so taken by Saint-Exupéry that he later incorporated the aviator's experiences into the repertoire of stories he told about *his own* life.

A close family friend told me my father started to make things up not long after the war, unashamedly appropriating the experiences of his best friend, Noel Howard, as an air force pilot. Why, still in his twenties, before his troubles with the law, did my father feel compelled to fabricate his life story?

It wasn't until I learned more about *his* father and grandfather that a pattern began to emerge. All three men had, in their youth, experienced war and violence and left their homes and crossed a sea to contrive a new future out of nothing. Identity and invention were intermingled from the very beginning.

My great-grandfather was about six years old when he was found, an orphan, on the streets of Damascus, Syria. I say "about" because he didn't know who his parents were or exactly what year he was born, much less his national or religious identity. He was one of thousands of children displaced in the aftermath of the massacres of the Maronites by the Druze in 1860.

Damascus, 1862

The violence and destruction of the civil war made headlines in Europe and America. It was followed by deadly pandemics and an economic cataclysm that scarred a city, already in decline, for years to come. When Mark Twain visited Damascus in 1867, the legendary desert oasis, once linked to the biblical Garden of Eden with its great palaces and mosques, had fallen further into decay and disrepair.

"It is . . . crooked and cramped and dirty. The gardens are hidden by high mud-walls and the paradise has become a very sink of pollution and uncomeliness." Twain described coming across naked boys with their hands out and "children in all stages of mutilation and decay." One of those boys on the streets was my great-grandfather, who wrote a letter about his childhood when he was in his eighties:

> *As far as I know about my origins, I [was] found in 1869 . . . by a missionary of the Fathers of Lazarus congregation. The missionary who, if my memory is right, was named Hujent or Najeau took me with him to Alexandria, Egypt, and placed me in an orphanage run by the Sisters of St. Vincent de Paul.*

At that time, the easiest, most traveled route to Egypt was to cross the modest mountain range that separates Damascus from the port of Sidon and to sail from Sidon to Alexandria. My great-grandfather had never seen the blue Mediterranean Sea, never been on a boat, never felt the salty breeze on his cheeks. This first sea voyage, leaving behind the mayhem and hardship of his early street existence, heading for a new life, inspired him and opened his eyes to wider horizons. Later, from the orphanage terrace gardens in Alexandria where he worked weeding vegetable beds and chopping wood, he would gaze out at the ships leaving the harbor in the distance and dream of becoming a sailor in the French navy.

On Christmas eve 1871, he was christened and given the name of Alfred Vincent. His last name (mine too) was taken from St. Vincent de Paul, the religious order that administered the orphanage. He had been fed, given a uniform, and taught to read and write French and Arabic. In his letter he wrote that the nuns were stern, perhaps worse. He left the institution as soon as he was allowed. At first he went door-to-door looking for odd jobs and sleeping wherever he found shelter. For a few months he worked and slept in a bakery. But most often he wandered the docks looking for work as a seaman. In June of 1879, having been turned down by the French navy (the French considered him a Turk, born as an Ottoman subject), he joined the crew of a commercial schooner loaded with lentils and sailed out of Alexandria harbor, bound for Europe. He was sixteen or seventeen years old. He wrote,

> *The voyage from Alexandria to Dunkirk, which took about 3 months, was full of ordeals. To start with, I was so seasick I lay on the hot deck for almost twelve days . . . without eating. Little by little I regained my strength and was able to weather the seas, as long as it didn't get too rough.*

He recovered by the time the ship reached the calm waters off Sicily; he saw giant sea turtles and whales breaching as they sailed past the Rock of Gibraltar. But he never got his sea legs, and once in Dunkirk, he renounced his ambitions to be a sailor. He made his way to Paris and eventually returned to North Africa, landing in Algiers, the glistening white port on the Mediterranean. Algeria was known for its relative tolerance of foreigners, including Christians, Jews, and "Turks." After years of selling carpets on the street, he became a modestly successful import-export merchant, and in 1893 he was finally granted French citizenship. By then he had a wife and two sons, and eventually his own home on a street high above the harbor with a view of the sea.

The violence and difficulties of his childhood, his very name, remained locked inside of him. Those that knew him said he was an enigma, distant, reserved; he kept his heart buried. When his wife, Rose, died unexpectedly at age forty, his mother-in-law, Pauline, a hardened, widowed colonialist, accused Alfred of poisoning her daughter. (Rose died of sepsis, a common occurrence at that time.) Pauline had never liked Alfred, who she described as a "Turkish carpet salesman who had grown up on government assistance." She later claimed, hysterically, that he tried to inject her, too, with poison at a market.

Two years after Rose died, Alfred's eldest son, his favorite, was killed in France during World War I. The younger son, my grandfather, also enlisted in the French army and was sent across the Mediterranean to the trenches in eastern France. His name was Arnold. To avenge his older brother's death, he took out a German machine gun nest in the battle of Serre and was awarded the Croix de Guerre. He returned to Algiers a war hero and married my grandmother, Marguerite, the daughter of well-off French colonialists.

At the end of World War I, the young couple moved in with Alfred, the widowed orphan, who gave his son the bedroom he had once shared with Rose. But it was an uneasy household. "Arnold's father is a bizarre man, full of complexes and resentments. He is mean and full of contempt," my grandmother wrote about Alfred in her diary. "He doesn't like me. His son annoys him. He complains constantly about his character." Alfred was obsessed with his business—his ledgers, counting tins of sardines, ounces of chocolate and percentages of profit. For Arnold, in front of his wife and well-off in-laws, his father's destitute origins and lack of education was embarrassing.

Author's grandparents, Arnold and Marguerite

Two years after Arnold's marriage to Marguerite, she gave birth to a son, Guy. In the months after my father's birth, my grandmother realized her husband, Arnold, was not well—that as much as he disdained his father, he had inherited his strange distance and disequilibrium.

My grandfather Arnold charmed people with his inviting blue eyes and iridescent smile, but he also exploded in anger for no reason; he was "constantly agitated." Marguerite thought it was the war, the early deaths of his mother and older brother. She would wait on the veranda with my father in her arms for

Arnold to come home for dinner, but she soon discovered my grandfather was having an affair. He swore he only loved her, that he would never deceive her again. She forgave him and kicked out a friend who tried to warn her that Arnold was a trickster, an aberrant neurotic who would ruin her life.

Arnold was arrested for a car accident that resulted in the injury of another person, then he got into a fight and was arrested again. His wine business, financed by Marguerite's family's money, collapsed. He forced her to have two abortions. The hemp factory he invested in burned down. He had another affair.

In 1926, after a bitter disagreement with his father about a business deal, Arnold decided to leave Algeria and his father for good. He moved Marguerite, who was pregnant, and my father, who was seven, to France. On the thirty-hour crossing from Algiers to Marseille, Marguerite went into labor, giving birth to a daughter, Suzel, as the boat waited in the harbor of Marseille to dock.

The family moved to Paris where Marguerite had another daughter, Arlette. Arnold's dreams magnified. It was the rollicking 1920s, and Paris was on fire. They acquired a large, dark apartment with high ceilings and a marble mantelpiece in the living room on Avenue Carnot near the Arc de Triomphe. Also in that apartment was a tall walnut chest of drawers with a marble top and a mirror. I know of it because that piece of furniture followed my grandparents to America and ended up in a corner of the apartment where I grew up. In it my father kept the family documents and photographs, and his private business papers. It was the family vault, the keeper of history and secrets.

No one in the family could tell me exactly what Arnold, my grandfather, did, but he seemed to have many businesses in Paris. I discovered some were financed with the help of Marguerite's father, Firmin Faure, a lawyer and a nationalist French deputy whose extremist rants once, a decade or more before, caused him to be escorted from the French National Assembly by armed guards. Faure had since become a dowser, a kind of "geologist" detecting water and valuable minerals underground using a divining rod, which he followed up with a fringe career in teleradiesthesy—using photographs and electrical impulses to divine a person's intelligence and character—hence perhaps my grandmother's interest in tarot.

In 1935, Arnold (who described his profession as a "engineer," or alternatively a "geologist," as did my father and Firmin Faure) was sentenced to three months in prison for a Ponzi scheme called "The House of Wisdom." His sentence was suspended, and then a few months later, in the spring of 1936, he offered 350,000 francs each to two of France's most famous actors, Yvonne Printemps and her partner, Pierre Fresnay, to star in a movie he was "producing" titled "Madame Bonaparte." That fantasy unraveled in lurches—there was no money, no director, and only half a script—and four years later, Arnold, sued by Printemps for fraud and breach of contract, was sentenced to four years in prison. By then he had been implicated in schemes involving bonds, arms sales, and ship building and was openly called a swindler in the French newspapers.

Meanwhile, at home, Marguerite decorated their apartment with French Empire "antique" furniture. There were thick, floor-length curtains, large vases filled with flowers, and a bulky radio by the fireplace. Arnold insisted the children be strictly brought up. My father was made to kneel on the floor beside his father like a choirboy—or an orphan—as he greeted dinner guests at the front door. The girls were sent to a private Catholic school. Arnold lectured the children on proper behavior and morality. Lying, he was fond of reminding his children with his trademark smile, was a sin.

Guy with his father and sisters

Looking at pictures of my father before World War II is confusing. In one photograph he's a beaming Boy Scout on his mother's arm; in another, a slick city kid wearing a double-breasted suit with pocket foulard, standing beside his father. There are other personalities: a lanky, effete teenager in his white tennis attire; a responsible older brother holding his younger sisters' hands as they walk down the street; and in one almost unrecognizable photo, a tight-lipped, Cocteau-like boulevard dandy.

He told me stories about sneaking out of the Avenue Carnot apartment at night, shimmying down the drainpipes from the second-floor balcony to "borrow" his father's car to drive to the clubs in Montmartre with his fencing partner and closest pal, Noel Howard. Noel was the son of a sculptor; he smoked and drew caricatures of the bohemian artists and writers in the cafés where they listened to jazz: songs like "Minor Swing" and "La Mer," played by Django Reinhardt and others by the likes of Fats Waller and Duke Ellington. The song "Sophisticated Lady" was on everyone's lips—the cafés' smoky, dark spaces filled with voyeurs and intellectuals, opium users, men and women in drag kissing, drinking, dancing, and not thinking much about tomorrow.

My father and Noel stayed up through the night, until morning shone on the damp cobblestone streets, the melodies and the lyrics of those songs sinking in deep. They became a part of my father. He hummed and recalled the lines word by word when he was in his eighties. "Oh, those were the days," he'd say.

In the last photograph I've found of my father taken before the German invasion of France, probably during the summer of 1939, he sits on the edge of the family circle—on a lawn—a grim, brooding eighteen-year-old about to enlist in the French army. Less than a year later, he was captured and, along with two and a half million other French soldiers, was taken prisoner by the Germans.

In September of 1940, my father escaped. According to one story, he hid in a pile of dead bodies in the back of a truck;

in another, he swam from France to Spain across the Bidasoa river. It's unclear if either account is true, but certainly the war had not gone the way he or his commanding French generals imagined. His father had emerged from World War I a victorious hero with a medal pinned to his chest. Guy was a refugee in his own country. He joined his family and an exodus of thousands fleeing the Germans as they crossed over into Spain (we have photographs of this). In Madrid, the embassy issued him a US visa and he traveled on to Lisbon, where he stood a part of the crush of disheveled ex-French soldiers on the dock, waiting to board the *Siboney*.

The Atlantic crossing was stormy (Saint-Exupéry retired to his cabin) but mercifully brief. Ten days later, on December 31, 1940, New Year's Eve, the *Siboney* arrived in New York Harbor. Saint-Exupéry was greeted by a bundle of reporters and photographers. My father, with a hundred dollars in his pocket, quietly entered the unfamiliar city and found his way to the Ambassador Hotel to wait for his family and start a new life.

CHAPTER 19

Gales and a Long-Beaked Bird

Thursday, April 14
N 35.27, W 39.44
457 miles to the Azores

We reached and passed north of the thirty-fifth parallel overnight, in rough weather.

> *This morning I woke up again into a developing gale, rain pouring, dense clouds, rising seas. The captain was at the helm, a mute, silhouetted dark shape against the sea, shackled to the lifeline, unapproachable.*

I scrunched up in a corner of the cockpit, at the top of the companionway, using the dodger (a canvas windscreen fixed to the top of the cabin) to keep the wind-driven pellets of rain off my face. We nodded and grunted a greeting. I'd heard a commotion on deck in the middle of the night, but I didn't want to ask what had happened. The boat was sharply heeled over, a white river of water streaming by the leeward rail. Steep waves surged under the stern of the boat, tipping us forward as we raced down their flanks. I kept my eyes on the anemometer so I would know the wind speed, direction, and our point of sail when the captain turned the helm over to me. We were in a close reach. The wind velocity was in the high twenties, occasionally gusting over thirty knots.

When the captain went below, he slammed shut the companionway hatch behind him to keep out the breaking seas. I was on my own again for an hour or two. My arms and legs were stiff from days of fighting brutish winds and steep waves. My fingers soon cramped from holding tight to the wheel. I kept checking my safety lines, afraid I might be swept off the boat, never to be seen again.

Later that morning, below deck, I was braced in the galley, using a mechanical pincer to keep a pot of water I was heating from sliding off the stove, when Yves came out of his cabin. He looked exhausted, stunned. I asked him how his night watch had gone.

"It was rough," he said. The turnovers at the helm with Nikos had not gone well. Nikos kept losing his bearings, the boat reeling this way and that until the captain arrived and had a fit. "It was traumatic," he said.

Traumatic? I had never heard Yves talk this way.

"I told Dimitri I can't do it anymore," Yves said.

"What?"

"I can't steer the boat with thirty-knot winds in a storm in the rain at night, with the clouds and no stars to tell me where I am. I told him I can't do it. I'm sorry, but next time, we need to put the autopilot on."

It was hard to believe. Yves rarely admitted to any physical limitations. He was obviously drained, reaching the end of his rope.

"I think I'm . . ." he hesitated. "I'm about ready to get off the boat in the Azores with you."

He lurched over to the galley and took control of the pot of hot water on the stove so he could make tea and shove a few crackers down his throat before starting his watch.

• • •

I went back on deck to wait for him to relieve my shift. The weather worsened. Another squall unleashed a torrent of rain and angry gusts over thirty-five knots. As soon as Yves came on deck—Nikos, too, had arrived—the captain, at the helm, ordered us back into action.

"Release the outhaul. Take in the main sheet!" the captain shouted.

I did what I was told, correctly, ducking as a wave crested and broke over us. But I was afraid, trying not to let my legs shake.

"Bring in the furling, release the jib sheet!" he commanded.

When Nikos pulled on the wrong sheet, Dimitri lashed out at him in Greek. The harangue went on until we had properly set the sails. A half hour later, as we coiled the lines in silence, the captain spoke again.

"Listen up, guys," His voice had taken on a lower, but more urgent tone. "It's important you focus now on what you have to do. No more mistakes." The careful way he enunciated each word was unnerving. He had announced we were entering a different realm—a level of heavy weather and high seas dangerous and challenging, even to an experienced captain like Dimitri.

Though I'd been on watch for more than three hours, Dimitri put me back behind the helm. At the moment, I thought he forgot I was off watch. Only later did I realize he didn't have a choice. Nikos had just flailed at the helm, Yves had drawn the line the night before. That meant if Dimitri didn't want to use the autopilot and drain the battery, he had to keep me at the helm as much as possible.

"You are the best at the wheel," he had told me sharply, perhaps inadvertently, days earlier when I tried to beg off helming with the spinnaker. "You can do it!"

It boosted my confidence that the captain trusted me under those conditions. I worried now he was overestimating my physical stamina. I was getting less sleep. My thoughts were blurry. My bones and muscles ached. I was feeling my age.

Luckily that morning the squalls became less frequent, and the winds fell into the midtwenties. I told myself that all I had to do was hold on another hour, and then I would just go below and sleep, no matter what the schedule.

Author at the helm

Thursday p.m. Another squall hit while I slept. Lurching like a drunk man in the dark, I fix a cup of tea, drink it, and climb back up the companionway steps to the deck. The last sunlight of the day. Streaks of light between the clouds and the cresting wave peaks. It appears that the worst of the series of lows may be behind us.

Before the captain goes below, I ask him if he thinks there are more gales on the way. I'd lost track if we'd been through two or three or more.

"I don't know. We will have to wait and see."

Yves and I are on watch when a large brown bird with a white breast and yellow duck-webbed feet lands on the solar panels above the helm. It has a long, sharp beak like a Venetian carnival mask and ice-blue eyes. It rocks back and forth trying to hold on to the bar as the boat lifts and falls. It, too, is very tired. As it grows dark, the bird glides down to the deck and finds a partially protected place on the cabin roof near the dodger. Yves dubs the bird "Henri."

Later, when the moon rises, Yves starts to croon like Sinatra, the well-known song about flying to the moon and frolicking among the stars.

When we reach the crest of a tall wave, the moonlight is spread out on a vast undulating plain of waves that continues to the horizon. Within three days we hope to land in the Azores.

CHAPTER 20

The Eye of the Storm

Friday 4/15
N 36.12, W. 35.49
Got some sleep last night after magical sailing
under the moon. . . . This morning I split the last
orange with Yves. Henri, the bird, is still alive.

Henri is a brown booby, common in the Caribbean and along the west coast of South America. Usually gregarious birds, they stay close to shore and return to land at night. Henri, though, has wandered more than a thousand miles from his usual territory.

First he squatted on the deck near the rail, then he hopped over the cabin to the windward side of the boat and stuck his head up, pointing his beak straight up into the sky. The captain told us that birds when they landed on a boat mid-ocean were often lost, exhausted, and had come to the boat to die. They were considered bad omens. But that morning, Henri, after looking up at the sky, suddenly spread his long wings and lifted into the air. Within seconds he was gracefully catching updrafts over the crest of the tallest waves, pivoting and gliding down the other side. I lost track of him and thought he was gone, but ten minutes later, perhaps after having caught a flying fish for breakfast, Henri was back on the cabin roof.

Unfortunately, the bird did bring with him some bad news.

I was on deck when the captain came up from below and told me a new low was developing between us and the Azores—now about five hundred miles away. We were also running out of our west winds that were blowing us toward the Azores. I asked him what we were going to do. He hunched his shoulders and shook his head as if it didn't matter. Either we continue our course, inevitably running into the new low, which he told me bluntly was developing into a tropical storm with winds above 35 to 45 knots, or we turn around and sail back west where we had come from.

The message was clear. We weren't going to retreat westward, so we were trapped. At the moment, though, it didn't seem that way. The sun had appeared between broken clouds and the seas were subsiding. In a way, the pleasant weather made the news harder to take, as if we were being punished for hoping the last storm was behind us; that our ocean crossing would be just another average, challenging, but manageable trip across thousands of miles of open ocean ending with a celebratory arrival in the Azores.

"Where is the low now?" I asked the captain.

"I don't know. It could open up right on top of us," he said.

I tried not to show my feelings, but I felt like I'd been hit by something way larger and more powerful than me. That I could not, in fact, do anything to avert this ending. That it was a question of fate. That we were, as I had feared, doomed all along. Or worse, that it was me who was cursed and had inflicted a spell on the boat.

"I'd like to call my wife," I said to him.

• • •

It was a beautiful spring day on Long Island, where Stacy was in line at the town clerk's office to renew the resident sticker for our car. We had not talked since our separation that rainy, windy morning on St. Martin. When she saw the call coming in, she hurried outside. It took us several tries before we connected on the satellite phone. I acted upbeat. We had gone through a patch of bad weather, I told her, but we had made good time. We could reach the westernmost Azores within three days.

"How are you?" she asked.

"I'm good. We're drying out some of our clothes this morning. How are you?"

"Good. Everything is fine at home."

We talked for a minute or two more, then I told her I had to get off the phone.

"I'll call you as soon as we arrive," I told her.

"I love you," she said.

"I love you too."

I thought I'd covered up my fears. (Stacy later told me she heard "hesitancy" in my voice.) It was good to hear her voice. It made everything seem so normal. Of course, everything was going to be alright. Stacy was renewing the car sticker. I would soon be back there, in the shingled saltbox that I cherished, with my writing shack in the back, nestled by trees, a ten-minute walk from the bay.

For much of that day, the tropical storm, wherever it was, seemed unreal, a bad dream, an incorrect forecast.

It wasn't until midafternoon that I noticed clouds gathering to the north and west of us. They were mostly behind us, I thought, tall cumulus clouds bubbling into the stratosphere. Then they spread to the south as well. And finally, as the afternoon lost its warm serenity, the clouds closed in on us from the east too. The one remaining patch of light in the sky was directly above us. We were sailing into the eye of the storm.

CHAPTER 21

Something Happened

Something happened to my father during the war. He didn't tell me this. I read about it in the panic-struck memoir of his first wife, Gael Elton Mayo.

In May of 1945, shortly after the declaration of VE Day in Europe, Gael arrived in Paris with their nine-month-old daughter, Guislaine. In some photos from that summer, Gael and Guy look sultry, still in love; in others, stunned, not sure how to hold hands anymore. In Paris, they strolled down the Boulevard Saint-Michel with their daughter, dodging pedestrians still hugging and celebrating the victory over Germany. In the evening, they went to Café de Flore near Saint-Germain-des-Prés crowded with revelers.

Their reunion, though, was a disappointment to Gael. Guy was "very pleased" to meet his daughter, she wrote, but "in his speech and attitude . . . he was a complete stranger." There was a dark side, a "cold brutality" she hadn't seen before. Who was "this new cynical fellow with rather sinister plans to get rich quick in peacetime?" she asked. "What happened to our lovely love?"

Gael had met my father on a date arranged by her former husband, a White Russian, in New York in the autumn of 1943. My father, she wrote, was funny, idealistic, and warm—doing entrechats on the curb like Charlie Chaplin. They fell in love and married the following summer, just before he left for officer training and was sent abroad with the US Army.

But by the end of the summer in France after the war, Gael had had enough. She packed her bags and returned to New York with Guislaine. Guy soon followed. For a few years they went back and forth across the Atlantic, sometimes living together, sometimes not. Gael soon realized her husband could not adapt to peace. He was too impatient to be a father or provide a steady home for their daughter, but he wouldn't let go of them either.

During the summer of 1946, they had a fight at a lunch with family and friends in the large house my grandparents rented (and could not afford) on the rocky shore of the Long Island Sound in Rye, New York. Gael was sitting next to a guest she had invited. She wanted to be a journalist (her father was a Harvard professor) and surrounded herself with influential men in literary and art circles. It irked Guy. When Gael's hand lingered too long on her friend's arm, it was more than he could handle. Guy dragged her from the table and beat her on the lawn until others intervened.

Years later, Gael's lawyers pointed to the incident in the divorce papers as an example of how my father had changed, of his sudden unpredictable moods and violent temper. For my grandmother, Guy's implosion had a sad inevitability to it. She was close to her son; she had cradled Guy as an infant in her arms on the veranda in Algiers in 1920, waiting for Arnold, *her* ex-soldier, violent, errant husband to come home. She had seen Arnold denigrated and belittled by *his* father. She lived through the consequences: the bitterness and resentment, the delusion and lies over the decades. Now it was all repeating.

Arnold was doing to Guy what his father had done to him. They were in a bitter conflict over a business deal. My grandmother tried to talk to my father. She tried to bring father and son together, but by then Guy hated his father as much as Arnold had despised his own.

In Rye, there were angry, teary scenes behind closed doors. My grandfather Arnold was having another affair, and his grandiose business projects inevitably blew up into disagreements with investors. He acquired an aristocratic-sounding name—Chastenet de la Maisoneuve—to make up for the ignominy of his orphan father, to cover up his criminality in France, and the lack of any real money or legitimate business in America. The great rambling shingle house, with its many chimneys and wings, the backdrop of many family photographs, that testament to my family's early success in America, was given up after 1947. The Vincent façade collapsed. My grandparents separated, on their way to divorce. My father's sisters married themselves off—the youngest one, Arlette, at sixteen. My father, stabbed in the back by his father in a shipping business deal that might have set him up for life, disappeared overseas for long periods of time. He was determined to make his own fortune, to rescue his mother from his father, to win Gael back, and to be the family provider. Tellingly, he is not in any of the family photographs at Rye I've seen, except one—a blurry image of him on a tiny inflatable boat, motoring in choppy water with the shoreline in the background.

The eerie prophetic thing is, if the camera had been turned 180 degrees, you would see, across the Long Island Sound, the distant white stretch of beach on Sands Point where I first launched my inflatable dinghy forty years later.

CHAPTER 22

Multiple Lives

We want to know who our *real* parents are. We hope they are heroes. We also want to know their dirty secrets. We wonder what they were like before they had us. How did they become adult, leading the way, like a captain, unquestionable even if they were untrustworthy?

I had two fathers. The one in front of me getting dressed late in the morning, tucking in the tail of his tailored shirt, folding his silk foulard into his chest pocket, warm, smelling of eau de cologne, zigzagging through traffic confidently, singing, being funny. And the man he was hiding from me.

My father told me—and anyone else who asked—that during World War II he was a pilot in the US Air Force. He was a navigator in "Black Widow" bombers over Italy and Germany. He was a parachutist who had been dropped behind the lines and had to fight his way back over to Paris. After the war, he confided, he was recruited into the OSS, the precursor to the CIA.

The transcripts of his US Army record, *which he gave me*, show that he was never in the American air force (though he did briefly train with a French air force division before the German invasion). He was given high marks for his proficiency in languages, his intelligence, and his way with the regular troops. It was suggested that he'd be good at propaganda, but if he was ever in the OSS or CIA there are no documents to verify it.

As I was growing up, it became clearer to me that his career as a spook was simply cover. Under the guise of patriotic duty any dubious activities, disappearances, brushes with the law, multiple passports—indeed, *any* discrepancies—could be explained away.

In London in the early 1990s, when I visited my half sister, Guislaine, I was relieved to find a piece of the truth. It was a yellowed, wartime clipping from the *Baltimore Sun* with a picture of my father in his officer's dress uniform and high cap, reviewing a row of soldiers at Fort Meade in Maryland.

Lieutenant Vincent was second in command of a special detachment of French soldiers training to join international forces overseas, the article said. My father was sent to North Africa, where he served as liaison officer and translator for the gathering Allied French, American, and British forces that were providing support for the invasion of Italy and preparing to land in southern France.

I have his gray cardboard army identification card, with a photograph as proof that he was there—that it really happened.

Another glimpse of my father during the war comes from a letter my great-grandfather, the orphan from Syria, wrote. In the early summer of 1944, Guy was posted to Algiers, his birthplace. One afternoon he knocked on Alfred's door, and his grandfather, who he had not seen since he was thirteen or fourteen, opened it.

Alfred took Guy in his arms. "I pressed him against my chest, hugging him with such force that I thought my heart would never be satisfied," Alfred wrote in the letter, which was addressed to his son, Arnold. "I was in such a state that I confused him with you. Obviously, it was an illusion."

Alfred was living alone; his second wife had left him years before and taken with her their two sons. In his long, rambling letter he tried to convince Arnold to move back to Algeria with Guy and the rest of his family and go into business with him. Guy's visit was brief. He left with the invading forces for France, and Alfred never saw his grandson again. He died in Algiers a year or two later in a country that, like Syria in 1860, was being engulfed in what would turn out to be a long, tragic, bloody civil war.

On occasion, having a late dinner with my father in an empty restaurant in New York, he'd reenact with relish the way he would salute his commanding officers. "Yes, sir!" He snapped his hand to his forehead. His missions for the "top brass," he confided to me, were often *on the q.t.* (he was proud of his American vernacular). The messages he carried between military commands were *strictly confidential*. His voice would drop to indicate the seriousness of this and then he would explode with a clap of false laughter. "Ha! Of course, this would sometimes involve requisitioning a jeep, finding somewhere a case of wine and tins of foie gras. Ha!"

I suspect he knew in the years following the war that these entertaining escapades were not war hero material. He had no medals to impress his father. He had the scar on his chin and a story about being ambushed on his way to Paris, but I'm not sure he ever had combat experience. The story he told to his pals at Harry's Bar in Paris, after the war, about flying over Germany was harmless braggadocio. At least he thought of it that way when he woke up hung over the next morning.

Over the years I realized it was what my father hadn't done in the war that ate away at him, contributing to a silent feeling of inadequacy and his erratic blowups. His war was, like that of many other soldiers, not particularly heroic or valorous. The hard truth, I received sotto voce from my father, was that survival on the battleground, in all its various iterations, involved cold-blooded decisions and deceit. It was not something you talked about, even if you wanted to. It was really nobody else's business, anyway. *Everybody* was a fucking hypocrite.

After the war, my father's mission was to survive, American style. That is, any way you could. If his projects fell short of success, he kept his chin up. On his postcards from the far corners of the globe, he drew a camel, at times laden with bags of treasure; at other times, limping along with a crutch. He endured, rummaging for the strength to reinvent himself again and again.

In 1966, after the gold mine in Ecuador didn't pan out, my parents separated, and my sister and I were sent to stay with friends (two actors) and their adopted children in California.

During the next fifteen years I rarely spent time with my father. An attempt to reconnect between high school and college in Paris, where he then lived with a new wife and a daughter, resulted in us not speaking. In between, he owned a limousine service and two restaurants—one in New York, one in Paris. He spent a year in and around Wichita, Kansas, selling a van with a swirling radar on the roof to detect oil deposits. He promoted the construction of a refinery in Nigeria. His transformations were impressive, almost magical, yet there was a sadness and peril (more debts, more run-ins with the law) to his existence. Odysseus-like, he moved from one metaphorical adventure to another, without ever, it seemed, reaching home.

He emerged in the 1980s in Los Angeles, with my *belle mère*, Annie, and younger half sister, Claudie. He had legally changed his name, years before, in a Colorado courthouse to Guy Chastenet, to which, like his father, he appended "de la Maisoneuve." It had a ring to it that appealed to the fun set in California.

In ten years he rented or owned six different homes, most in Beverly Hills, with the same leased white Mercedes-Benz in every driveway. He had a satellite phone he carried in a suitcase to lunch at Ma Maison (*the* place to dine in LA at the time). He still threw good parties, where his friends danced waist to waist, clustered about him, in a tangy cloud of French eau de cologne.

By then I had graduated from Harvard. Most of my college tuition had been paid for by a work scholarship program in which I was employed first as a janitor in senior dorms and then a stage carpenter and lighting technician at the American Repertory Theater (which had moved from Yale to Harvard).

I was also writing plays, the first, *Alex*, winning a prize and a production in Cambridge. I'd been intrigued by the theater ever since I'd stood as a child in the darkness of the backstage wings, watching the make-believe on stage captivate an audience. I was brought up around different identities, fictional and otherwise (my mother's performances on- and offstage, my father's reality-altering moods and lies), so it seemed normal to me that an actor or anyone could be more than one person at once. Theater, where reality is always at play, seemed a natural place for me to be. After graduation I moved to San Francisco where I wrote one-acts and worked at the Magic Theatre where Sam Shepard's *Fool for Love* was premiering.

When I visited my father in Los Angeles, he took me to a building downtown. We stood in the middle of a floor-wide office for a legendary but defunct American engineering firm. I listened politely while my father explained that this was now *his* company; it had a contract to build a futuristic city in Saudi Arabia. He showed me the plaque on his corner office door that read "Guy Chastenet, President."

"Wow!" I was still playing cheerleader for his team of one.

There was a small model of the desert utopian capital on a table, but otherwise no desks, chairs, or anything or *anyone*, as a matter of fact, in the office. Not even a receptionist. Just an expanse of wall-to-wall carpeting and a phone on the floor plugged into a jack.

Like father, like son: the pall of being an imposter shadowed me for a long time. I moved back to New York to a storefront on the Lower East Side, 9th Street between C and D. My leather-jacketed superintendent in the next-door ground-floor apartment kept his Harley-Davidson inside his main room (my motorcycle was chained outside). My neighbor upstairs was the dominatrix of the New York club Danceteria. Across the street, homeless punks, some with shaved heads, other with mohawks, lived in an abandoned, windowless building—using the fire hydrant to wash.

I wrote during the day and drove a cab at night. Then I landed a job as an editor and reporter at a nonofficial United Nation's newspaper. On the side, a few of the plays I'd written were produced—black comedies about the end of '60s idealism: abused waitresses; evangelical, drug-addicted bikers; polyamorous professors. I had an agent at ICM. I worked with young Hollywood stars at the Actors Studio, but Off-Broadway theater did not pay the bills. I turned to teaching and then, finally, back to journalism. In the end, distinguishing fact from fiction became my profession and raison d'être.

By then I had met Stacy, a beacon of optimism in my noirish existence, and we married a few years later.

My relationship with my father remained unresolved. I still expected something from him—some love, which he gave me; some truth, which it turned out he could not face. When he had a heart attack and was in the hospital after triple bypass heart surgery, I went out to Los Angeles and held his waxy hand in the ICU. I looked at his intravenous-poked, monitored body behind the tent. I did not think he would survive.

Two months later I was in the desert with him, forty miles from the Arizona border where he was engineering a placer gold mine. He took me for a ride in a Ford Bronco to visit one of the test pits they had dug. It was hot and the truck smelled of gasoline and oil. The bare metal floor burned beneath my sneakers. The shift clanked as my father shoved the stick into third gear. I was reminded of Ecuador, of the blue Chevy truck, the dogs, too, and the snow-capped Andes outside the window. But I didn't say anything. I couldn't ask him what had happened to that mine (much less the marriage to my mother). I couldn't openly ponder what went wrong with so many of my father's projects because my job was to be a believer. He was a gold-mining engineer—the owner of an honest-to-goodness mine with bulldozers and sluice machines and corporate headquarters in a sparkling office building in Century City. I was there to protect him, not to uncover the discrepancies that would inevitably kick him in the ass . . . again. That was the problem. And because of the paradox of having to believe, dissemble, and protect *him* from the truth, there was this strange, awful silence a lot of the time between us that somehow I construed to be my fault.

That day, he kept driving farther into the desert, over hills and down gulches until we got caught in a dry riverbed of soft sand. He tried to escape, but he spun the wheels too long, only digging us in farther. We climbed out of the Bronco, and he slammed the door very hard, as if the door had done something terribly wrong. We looked around. Nothing but cacti and ocher dust with the sun burning above us.

The pits were proof positive there was gold in the dirt, a certain amount per X tons of dirt and gravel, presented with graphs and photos in the prospectus. But the piece of the puzzle missing, in this case, was water. Thousands of gallons of water per hour were needed to run through the machine, to rush down the sluice separating valuable gold from dirt.

It was not the first time I realized my father didn't think clearly about what he was doing. His entrepreneurship—and engineering—was a performance he winged his way through. He had a business card. He dug test pits.

That day in the desert, we did not walk back to the camp the long, safe way via the dirt road we had come on. Instead, he struck out across the hot desert. Despite the intervening hills, he said he knew exactly where the camp was. We walked in silence, in the heat of midday, without any water. I worried he might have another heart attack, but he kept trudging up one hill after another, humiliated and too angry at himself to know what to say to me.

Eventually the investors dried up and my father had to move again. His wife left him. He was arrested for passing bad checks. My sister, who had studied painting at Sarah Lawrence and married and would soon have children, bailed him out, and my father moved into a small, dark, one-bedroom rental in Santa Monica. He ended up alone, like his father and his grandfather.

At night he still went out to his favorite restaurant or to hear jazz, particularly big band jazz from the swing era. My niece and a younger cousin, then living in Los Angeles, would accompany him. He wore a wide-brimmed hat, a blue silk jacket with black velvet collar, a long scarf, and a skullcap ring on his finger. He would pick up an empty chair and dance with it up in the lights in front of the stage. "It's just one, one of them crazy things," he would bellow.

At home he fell into depression. He stuffed his overdue bills into garbage bags. Puddles of flax seed oil (he had prostate cancer) hardened on the refrigerator shelves and the kitchen counter. I found a few "poems" he wrote in 1994 and 1995, when was in his midseventies.

Empty Night
Walking silent streets
In the stillness of the night,
Lonely as a lost animal
Seeking a loving master . . .
I am cold, a rock of numbness
Bewildered . . .

He'd wake up the day after writing the poems to cross out lines and rewrite them in a more happy-go-lucky, upbeat tone, adding lines from favorite songs like "I'm in Heaven." He wrote one poem titled "Who Am I?" in a takeoff of the Sinatra tune "That's Life" about getting up after being smacked down. It was like DIY therapy.

I'm a friend and a soldier
A king and a pauper
A drinker and a saint wrapped in one!

I'm a priest and a peasant,
A camel and, just as pleasant,
The Devil's soul whose day has just begun!

He bought a revolver, and he wrote drafts of suicide notes addressed to us, his children, who were by then paying his rent.

CHAPTER 23
Sincerity

My father didn't shoot himself. He was too much of a sensualist. Not believing in an afterlife, he wanted to get all he could here on earth. He even held out hope for redemption of the materialist kind. He'd met a kind older man named Fred, a retired engineer living in New Jersey, who believed in his new ideas: the needle incinerator, the portable garbage recycling plant. Fred withdrew money from his retirement savings account to pay for engineering plans and mock-ups. Contracts were signed. My father, in his late seventies, still based in Santa Monica, made trips to Miami, Las Vegas, and Paris looking for investors. He sometimes ended up on the pull-out couch in Stacy and my tiny walk-up apartment on the far West Side. Fred would call me to ask when my father was arriving. Or he would call after my father had left and say he was sorry to hear my father was sick and couldn't make it to their planned meeting. He hoped he would get better soon.

On one of my father's visits, I took him to a neighborhood restaurant. We sat at the bar. There were the checkered-clothed tables in the background, the jazzy lounge music. The first drinks poured. It was all so familiar. Suddenly I couldn't bear the idea of hearing the same old stories and lies. I asked him about being in prison. It was the first time I admitted I knew what had happened the year I was born. He turned cold and distant, looking at me silently, like I was his most bitter enemy, the frightening stranger Gael had written about. He could never admit he had done anything wrong. "I know. You think I'm a crook," he said, then he stood up from the barstool and walked out the door.

In the end, Fred forgave him, as did many of the people he "borrowed" money from. I did too, but that was not enough. He wanted me to be his ally—and his alibi. At one point he asked me—as *his* father had done to him—to sign papers saying I was president of a new company he was forming. When I delicately declined, he wrote to say I was not his son. There was another interlude when we didn't talk. The years went by.

In his eighties, my father moved back to Paris into an attic apartment on the right bank. He drove a battered green Mustang Mach 1 to his favorite restaurants and bistros, some of the same places he had frequented when he was a teenager in the 1930s. The back seat was piled high with unpaid parking tickets, bills, and old newspapers and magazines. The parking valets treated him with hard-pressed *bonhomie*. He was the regular, the eccentric old guy who knew the maître d' and the piano player. For a time, he had a pretty "girlfriend" who held his arm and leaned her head on his shoulder. He sat at the same corner table, catty-corner to the banquette with the plaque "Sartre's Seat."

At home he fed the pigeons who landed on his balcony. One night, on Ambien, he wandered into the street in his pajamas. Another night, he was naked.

My sisters and I pooled our resources and reserved him a room in a comfortable, tidy nursing home outside Paris.

Walking on my arm toward the entrance for the first time, he stopped in his tracks. "When I come out of here it will be feet first." He looked at me terrified, then moved on solemnly, like a sentenced prisoner.

I saw him a few more times. Once in a hospital, I sat in his room as he slept, his lungs pausing their hard work longer and longer between breaths. When he woke up, he held my hand. He told me, as he often did in the last few years of his life, that he loved me, that I was a good son and he was proud of me (he did not want to repeat what his father and grandfather had done). He told me he'd had a dream. He listed all his "inventions," all his near successes.

"I was so close," he said.

I went to the window, which had a view of Paris in the distance. I told him it was a beautiful day outside.

"Oh, the fucking blue sky!"

"I'm going to make a phone call," I said. "Do you need anything?" He shook his head. I moved to the door and was about to close it when he spoke.

"More time," he said.

• • •

At the top of a closet, in a leather briefcase, are papers and photographs of my father's that I have not yet thrown out. Among them are two letters from his lawyer, dating to the early 1990s, attesting to Guy Vincent's legal stewardship of a ninety-five-foot mahogany-and-teak-adorned ketch (a sailboat with two masts, the mizzen or aft-mast smaller than the main). It is a stunning multimillion-dollar yacht, which was owned, in truth, by a good friend of his, the proprietor of a Parisian night club who deeded the yacht, called *Sincerity*, to my father for tax purposes.

Sometime in the early '90s, as payback, the owner of *Sincerity* lent my father the boat—and crew—for a couple of weeks. My father invited my newly rewed sister and husband to come to Saint-Tropez and join him for a honeymoon cruise with friends to Sardinia. I was also invited but declined. I was going through a difficult time in New York, trying to salvage my marriage and career. Unlike my grandfather and father, though, I had the advantage of therapy to help me understand what was broken and get me through a difficult time in my life. I also had an honest 8 a.m.-to-3 p.m. job with a weekly paycheck. It wasn't glamorous but it provided me with a sense of purpose. At the High School of Music & Art and Performing Arts, a public school, I did what I could to help inspire inner-city kids to surmount their own damaged childhoods. There were many boys in my classroom with absent fathers, with feelings of inadequacy and despair, with mothers struggling to pay the bills.

On the weekends I was beginning to fish, to go to the sea for succor. Perhaps I had already bought my first inflatable, I don't remember. But the luxury-yacht experience in Saint-Tropez was not for me. *Sincerity*, to me, was a play at sailing, a parody of what a sailor or a captain was supposed to be in place of the experience itself. I was trying to get to that essence, to learn how to navigate and cope with the vicissitudes of the wind and waves (as well as monthly bills and the demands of a regular job), to *not* repeat the delusionary performances of my antecedents.

My sister went and had a good time (and years later fell in love with sailing too). There were other guests on board, elaborate dinners cooked by my father, and music and dancing into the night. My father was happy. Why shouldn't he have been? It was a fantasy, a borrowed dream come true—to be a man of his word, the captain of his ship, the master of his destiny.

He died a year after I visited him in the hospital. On February 21, 2011, he woke up, wheeled himself to the nurses' station, and asked what the date was. Then he rolled back down the hall and watched his room fill with daylight. He looked at the toy Bugatti on the shelf, the cartoon drawings from his friends, the stuffed camels. He didn't make any noise or fuss. When the nurse came in a short while later with his breakfast, he was dead.

There's nothing like a parent's sparsely attended funeral, on a cold rainy morning, to remind you that you are on your own. Even if my father had rarely been there to be relied on, there was always the hope that he might be. That wish was like a ghost I'd see in every man I came to know or rely on, even if only briefly—a stranger giving me directions on the road, a fly-fishing guide teaching me how to cast on a riverbank. The absence of a guiding hand was a thorn in my side driving me to become more self-reliant, to stitch together fact and sentence, to double-check every source, to teach myself how to build a table, to tie knots, to tack into the wind, to navigate under the stars and, yes, to face my ultimate challenge—to cross the North Atlantic. All I needed was a trustworthy captain to show me the way.

CHAPTER 24

Sixty-knot Winds

It was so dark all I could see were the breaking seas at the stern of *Orion* and the clumps of white sea-foam flying by. The captain was standing at the helm, shackled to the safety line. His jacket was saturated, slick as a seal's coat. His face and hair were drenched as wave after wave broke against the side of the boat, showering him in water.

"Go below!" he yelled at me. "Shut the companionway!"

I looked at Nikos, who was hunched over the cockpit bench with his hands clasped in his lap. He nodded at me, to show me he was okay.

I closed the companionway hatch just as another wave broke above my head and lowered myself down the ladder into the main cabin. It was calmer down there, but the floor was slick with water and littered with pots and pans, plastic coffee cups, seat cushions. The ceiling hatches were leaking. Every few minutes when a wave crashed on the deck above, a stream of water would erupt from one corner of the companionway hatch.

I braced and pulled myself, in strategic lunges, over to the couch behind the saloon table and tried to half sit, half lie down. But the couch cushion wanted to slip under the table—piled now with every loose item in the cabin—and there were rivulets of water dripping on me from the ceiling. The wind clamored like a deranged child. The walls shuddered. The hull was whacked by waves as the bow heaved up and down. It couldn't get much worse, I figured, before we had to take emergency steps—lock ourselves into the boat and pray to God.

Earlier that day we had tried to skirt the low by sailing farther northeast. I was in the cockpit, trimming a sail, when the captain strode to the foredeck and picked up the dying booby bird. I thought he was going to hurl Henri overboard. Instead, he coddled the shivering bird in his arms, carried him to the stern, and carefully placed him in a sheltered spot behind the wheel. It was a signal by the captain that conditions were getting worse, sharper gusts of wind, steeper seas. It was also a deeply reassuring gesture to me. I finally realized at that moment that Dimitri would not abandon us. He *would* stay on deck for as long as it took to see *Orion* through the storm, a massive tropical depression we were still hoping to escape.

Unhappily, the winds kept rising, and by darkness, a ferocious storm with face-stinging gusts above forty-five and fifty knots had enveloped us. At some point, without any of us noticing, Henri died and was swept into the cold black ocean, a bundled rag of feathers and bone.

Down below, I felt helpless. I wanted to be on deck, but the captain had made the only decision he could. Any crew-member on deck was in danger of being swept off the boat by a breaking wave, and not one of us had the experience necessary to be deemed essential and worth the risk. At least Nikos spoke the same language, critical during the height of the storm when it was hard to understand what someone was yelling a few feet away. For Dimitri, Nikos, with his unquestioning obedience, was like having a third arm.

As for Yves, he was cuddled in the dry cocoon of his cabin, crammed between the folded sails and cushions, deep asleep. Yves's ability to ignore the circumstances around him baffled and infuriated me. He was a die-hard optimist. Everything was always fine to him, even if it wasn't. It's an admirable quality to have, I thought bitterly, until suddenly it isn't tenable.

I credited Yves's strength and insularity to his childhood, which, he told me, was enviably stable. His father was a hard worker, a regional director of a well-known French oil company, and his mother tended the house. They spent family summer vacations in Corsica, bouncing across Mediterranean-blue coves in an inflatable Zodiac (Yves was one of the few friends who appreciated and loved inflatables). The family had a house in Normandy that they still own. Yves left at seventeen, sailed across the ocean, traveled into the jungles of Guyana, and ended up in New York. In those days, many of us wandered at a young age, but Yves, except for visits, never moved back to France. I sensed there was something he didn't want to return to, but Yves never elaborated on what it might be. He did say his father was a hard nut to crack. In his eighties, confined to a wheelchair, he took his shotgun, balanced it between his knees, and blew his head off in the living room in Normandy.

"It was a statement," Yves allowed. "He could've easily rolled himself outside or to the garage." It was left up to Yves to fly over from New York and clean the blood and bits of brain off the walls.

I was braced at the saloon table and Yves was still asleep when the companionway flew open. "We're going to tack! Secure the navigation equipment on the chart table!" the captain yelled.

He slammed closed the hatch and I heard him hollering at Nikos to pull in what headsail we still had up. I slid over to the chart table where Dimitri's gaffer-taped laptop, an iPad, satellite phone (our only form of communication with the outside world), shortwave radio, and cell phone were scattered in a mess with extra headlamps, chargers, batteries, a video camera, and other odds and ends.

"Hey, Yves!" I called out. "Yves, fucking wake up!!"

It was too late. The captain tacked as we rose up the steep side of a wave and I was suddenly thrown about ten feet across the wet floor into a head door, the handle digging into the middle of my back. I cried out in pain, but I didn't have time to think about how bad I might have injured my back. The laptop had tumbled and was dangling by a cable banging the table and bench. While I clambered back across the slippery floor to retrieve it, Yves, finally awake, rushed to try to help me secure the rest of the equipment, which had slid against the chart-table guardrail and was threatening to cascade onto the floor. For several minutes we stood there, frozen, bracing ourselves and the equipment. The boat had swung around and was now leaning the other direction. We were at a sharp angle, the floor wet and slippery. There didn't seem to be a way out.

"Disconnect the cables and put the equipment in Nikos's berth," Yves suggested.

While one of us stayed at the chart table, arms spread out to stop the stuff from falling, the other disconnected and carried the equipment, one handful at a time, to Nikos's cabin. In a few minutes we had transferred everything to his berth and wrapped them in his sleeping bag, but the bandaged laptop, which housed our AIS system (the ability, among other things, to see and track ships in our path), we later realized, had been irredeemably damaged.

The hatch opened again and Nikos stepped slowly, stiffly, down the stairs. He was wet, rigid with cold, his pupils wide from the darkness on deck. He needed water. He needed to warm up. He was hungry. I stumbled to my cabin to find the remaining fruit-and-nut bars that Yves had given me weeks before and I had stashed in the bottom of my bag. None of us had eaten in ten hours. I gave a few to Nikos, then I climbed up the stairs and shoved the companionway roof back. The wind and the waves immediately knocked me to one side of the cockpit. I shackled to the lifeline and reached across the cockpit to hand the captain a few bars. He ripped the wrapping off one with his teeth and bit into it quickly, so as not to let go of the wheel as we rose above the crest of another wave. He managed a slight smile, a nod of thanks. For a moment we stood there like twin statues, pelted by the elements. I wanted to stay, but he did not need my help. He had spent his life preparing for this moment; he was determined and confident. He was going to save his boat.

I went back down below and joined Nikos and Yves, who were braced at the bottom of the companionway, staring up at the raging storm. It was clear to each of us only one question mattered: How long could the captain stand at the helm and guide *Orion* through the mayhem?

CHAPTER 25

Losing Control

The first night of the storm went on and on. The nonstop clamor of the wind. The violent shuddering of the mast. The percussionist thud of the waves against the hull. The dizzying movement up and down and side to side. We did not sleep. I prayed the captain would be able to hang on at the helm. I prayed that the winds would subside. Twenty-four hours later, I jotted down a few notes.

> *The captain and Nikos stayed on deck in the storm for most of the night and morning. After it was light, the captain came in once to attempt to get a weather update. He stood at the foot of the companionway dripping wet. Humbled. He told Yves and me that in all his years of sailing, he had never experienced such high winds—over 60 knots (almost 70 miles per hour).*

Many non-sailors do not realize that when wind speed doubles, say from ten knots to twenty knots, the *force* of the wind on the sails and the water quadruples so that it feels more like what you would expect at forty knots. And at forty knots, more what you would expect at 160 knots and so on. That night, on board *Orion*, we sailed into Beaufort-scale force 10 winds—force 12, a hurricane, being the highest on the scale. The Beaufort scale, created in 1805 by Admiral Francis Beaufort and used ever since by navies around the globe, defines force 10 as a "storm" with forty-eight- to fifty-five-knot winds and twenty-nine- to forty-one-foot waves "with overhanging crests, [the] sea white with densely blown foam." We were, it seems, for a few hours in the vortex of a force 11 "violent storm" with wind gusts of fifty-six to sixty-three knots and "exceptionally high waves."

The captain, in the blog posted more than twenty-four hours later and read by our wives and family at home, put it in less terrifying terms. "After thirty-six hours of perturbations that were challenging and in which the wind turned in our face and much stronger than what the forecasts said, the wind has now dropped to thirty knots (just below gale force) and we are always traveling upwind, with a little mainsail and staysail." The accompanying color-coded weather map showed our sailboat, represented by a small dot, located in the swirling red-purple zone centimeters from the eye of the storm.

In fact, we had not gone steadily upwind but zigzagged back and forth for thirty-six hours in dangerously high winds trying to find a way out of the storm.

Around 1 p.m., when the winds subsided to between thirty and forty knots, Nikos made a video. The dodger had been smashed, the still-cresting waves crashed against the deck, the wind kept up an eerie insistent aria, and the halyards banged against the mast. A voice calls out and no one answers.

It appears we have weathered the worst of the storm. The captain put the helm on autopilot and came down into the cabin for "lunch"—pieces of packaged toast smeared with chunks of Camembert cheese and some slices of dried sausage that Yves and I prepared. There was light in the sky and we were smiling. We applauded the captain's tenacity. It seemed a miracle we were still floating and alive.

The captain ate ravenously, but he was in no mood to rest. Believing the brunt of the storm had passed south of our location, he immediately ordered us to set off on a new course back upwind, northeast, toward the Azores and, it turned out, into the lingering storm. Four grueling hours later, it was dark again and the winds had only gotten worse.

We were sailing, heeled over, tight to the wind, crashing into waves at full speed. When Yves and I were not on deck, beaten by the wind and sea, we tried to rest below. For me, it was pointless. I didn't have a dry berth. The main cabin was still a mess, with the couch cushions, pots, empty liter plastic bottles of water rolling on the floor, the skylight hatches still leaking. The tail of the storm battered the boat hour after hour. The mast vibrated in the heavy wind; the cabin bulkheads cracked under pressure. Then a new disturbance pushed me to the brink.

Every time the boat came down hard on a wave, the hull directly below my berth would bang metallically, as if a mallet were hitting a sheet metal drum. For hours I ignored it and so did the captain. Finally, after a particularly loud crash, I heard him curse. He rushed into my cabin, tore off the mattress, and pulled up the board covering a hatch. He peered down into the bilge with a flashlight, looking to see if there was water below. Seeing little or none, he indicated with a wave of his hand that it was all okay. But to me, it was not okay. Far from it.

Though the captain had gained my trust, the leaks and relentless banging under my berth belittled my faith in the boat itself. Now I knew that in addition to the leaking sail locker in the bow, sloshing with water from the storm, and the dripping hatches in the cabin roof, there was a seventy-five-gallon steel water tank loose in the bilge. I had read about multimillion-dollar racing yachts breaking up—delaminated decks separating from hulls, bulkheads cracking, masts collapsing—in similar seas. I imagined the bolts of the water tank, sheared in the turbulence, being pounded into the fiberglass hull until it split open like a badly nailed coffin. In my mind, the old boat, driven by captain-fucking-Ahab at full force into the waves, would soon break up on its own.

I wrote in my journal,

> *I was not in good shape. The captain had turned on his shortwave radio (the satellite phone, which had to be*

on deck for reception, was useless in these conditions) searching for weather information. The whirring white noise, the constant banging on the hull, the exhaustion from holding on at a twenty-five-degree angle, the lack of sleep, and the threat of the never-ending storm was getting to me. I was physically shaking and beginning to lose it.

After more than two weeks of being stoic, of being manly, I was fighting the urge to crawl into a ball and cry. I could not and would not do that, but I had to do something. Nikos and I were repacking our life vests (for the twentieth time) in the darkness (the captain had turned off the cabin lights to preserve the batteries), prepping for our next watch, when I asked the captain if we could further reef the sails, just for an hour, so we could clean up the cabin and gather our thoughts. I pointed out all the water and debris still on the floor. I told him we were all exhausted. I had fallen and hurt my back. Yves had possibly fractured a rib and his thigh was turning purple. Nikos, too, had hurt himself. Dimitri looked at me with a bemused (and I thought condescending) smile. "We cannot take down the sails and keep moving in these seas," he said. I felt Nikos sitting, braced, in the darkness beside me, watching warily for the outcome of this confrontation.

"*Reef* the sails, not take them down," I reiterated stonily. "We need to slow down. We need to take a break."

He looked hard at me. "It is not possible," he said.

After my watch, I found a not-too-wet corner of my berth, closed the door, stuck a large cushion between me and the downwind bulkhead, held on to the heart rock Stacy had given me, and fell asleep, briefly, for the first time in two days. When I woke up in the middle of the night, Yves was there in his gear. I could sense from the movement of the boat and his expression that something had changed. He looked relieved. He told me he and Nikos had set up a new watch schedule.

Sometime after I left the deck, the captain changed his mind, eased off the wind, set sail for the southeast, and put *Orion* on autopilot. Traveling with the wind partially behind us and only a bit of sail left up, the boat leveled. The water tank in the hold stopped banging. The bulkheads were still. Except for the wind whistling outside and the creaking as we rose and fell over the rolling sea, the boat was quiet. The captain finally went down to his cabin and slept—on and off for the next twelve hours. We were at peace. The storm was not yet done lashing us, but we had capitulated and in doing so, we had won.

CHAPTER 26

Almost There

Monday 4/18
N 35.29, W 30.35

Sometimes being close to land is harder than being far away. It's like sitting before a plate of food but not being able to eat it. We were only about 250 miles from the nearest Azores island, but it was dead upwind of us. We had to tack to one side and then the other, in a zigzag motion. It was very slow going.

I spent much of this afternoon at the helm facing 25 knot winds, 6–10 ft seas. Some sun. Scattered clouds. Occasional squall. We didn't see a tanker crossing a ½ mile behind us for which we were reprimanded by the captain. That eve he let us know, reluctantly, that his AIS tracking software on his taped-up laptop was not working. We would not be warned of 300-foot container ships steaming for us at 20 knots at night just as we were entering a high-traffic area—nor would they see us. "You must look all the time," the captain told us.

Vigilance. Avoid collision. At this moment in the voyage, after the repeated gales and the punishment from the storm, my newfound patience and grace-under-pressure was wearing thin. I was weary. I just wanted to get off the boat as quickly as possible. Pressed against my cabin wall at night, my mattress and sleeping bag still sopping wet, not being able to sleep, time crawled by. My cabin was near the bow of the boat, and the pounding from the waves was more severe than Dimitri's and Nikos's sedate, dry cabins in the stern. I worried about a collision and the water tank beneath me, which had resumed banging against the hull. I had to calm myself and not dwell on hypothetical catastrophes. I focused on us getting there, on arriving, on how close we were, but our slow progress was excruciating. Going up on deck for my next watch, I checked the chart plotter (a digital chart showing our position). In eight hours we had only advanced sixteen miles toward our destination. We were moving at a speed two-thirds that of walking.

Tuesday 4/19
N 37.25, W 29.30
According to our original itinerary, we were supposed to have arrived today, but the storm set us back more than a hundred miles and now, in a light breeze, we are only moving at 4–5 knots. Yves covered the first hour of my shift and let me sleep an extra hour until 8:30.

When I woke up, Yves seemed to be in a daze, sitting at the saloon table, reading the *Atlantic Islands Pilotage Guide*. He had it open before him like the Bible. "It is very informative, nicely illustrated too. I highly recommend it," he said without irony. He began to read passages aloud. "Such and such sail maker and marine provisioner provides many services: launch pickup, pump-outs, power and water, haul-outs, engine and sail repair, replacement electronic equipment available . . ." Yves was on autopilot. He read aloud about hotels, restaurants, car rentals, and places to visit on the islands. He was all set to get off the boat and discover the Azores with me, though he still had not informed the captain or his wife, who would soon be waiting for him in Spain.

We still have 180 miles to go. The plan is to head north until we draw close to the coastlines of Faial and Pico Islands and then tack eastward about 150 miles to São Miguel. Seas permitting, at that point, the engine could really help save time. But I thought I heard the captain crank the engine a couple of times yesterday and I'm not sure if it started. Perhaps it was the generator that he was having a hard time with . . .

On deck later in the morning, the captain confirmed that we may not get into Ponta Delgado until late tomorrow night or the next morning.

"It's important today to stay close to the wind, you understand?" He looked at Yves, who was at the helm. "Otherwise we will never get there."

He was being rhetorical. But given the circumstances and what we had been through, the words weighed heavily on me. In my dinged-up brain, not ever getting to the Azores had become a real possibility.

• • •

I was at the helm most of that afternoon, sailing in an easy breeze with moderate chop and gray skies. It was about an hour before dusk when I thought I saw the steep dark shape of a volcano rise from the sea.

"I see land," I told Yves.

"Where?" he said. "I don't see anything."

It was the moment I had waited so long for, but it lacked conviction. In the low, misty light, it was hard to tell if the land existed since the island, if it was one, was camouflaged by clouds. It took a half hour, as we slowly approached, to determine if the cone shape was truly there or a mirage.

"It must be Pico," I said.

Mount Pico rises from the depths of the sea to nearly eight thousand feet, the tallest peak in Portugal. If you measure it from the ocean bottom, it's one of the highest mountains in the world. Yves and I quietly high-fived, but we did not cheer or jump around. In twilight, the volcano was ominous and inhospitable. It was easy to understand with what caution and fear explorers approached unknown shores in earlier times. Their imaginations conjured up mythological beasts, a one-eyed cyclops, Amazonian warriors. Or, as bad, they had to turn away from a wave-dashed shoreline of volcanic cliffs, no inviting coves to protect them, no fruit trees or fresh water.

"We have to tack," our captain said. He had come on deck to have a look. He waved at the land. "Goodbye, Pico."

In the gathering darkness, we tacked eastward, heading to our destination, the island of São Miguel, still 150 miles away.

CHAPTER 27

Midnight

Wednesday 4/20
N 37.33, W 27.37

It was after my first evening watch. I had not yet gotten to sleep in my damp, clammy berth when the wind died. The boat stopped moving forward. It tipped back and forth slightly, like a plastic toy boat in bathwater. I heard the captain come up from his cabin and, soon after, the welcome rumble of the engine.

In the morning, the sun came out and the winds stayed low, with a few passing clouds. After lunch, we sat stunned by the warm, still air, the clear sky, the peaceful sea.

"Yves, do you want a café?!" Nikos yelled out from the companionway.

"Is the pope Catholic?" Yves answered, half-asleep.

Nikos popped his head up, looking bewildered.

"Is the pope Catholic? What does it mean?"

We continued to motor all day, mile after mile. We brought all the cushions and mattresses out on deck to dry. We hung our wet clothes on the rails. We crushed the plastic water bottles into bags of garbage.

It was late in the afternoon when I saw the faint coastline of São Miguel, about twenty-five miles away. I told Yves and

Nikos. For a while we just stared at the shore to make certain it was there.

"We made it," Yves said.

The captain was nonplussed. "Okay," he said with a smile and went below. I dug into the refrigerator box for a cold beer. We got out crackers, cheese, and nuts. Yves and I toasted our arrival as Nikos took a picture of us.

For the first time in three weeks we had cell service. We were considering a call to our wives when we heard the engine falter. At first it was a hardly noticeable drop in rpm, but it soon repeated itself again. The captain hopped on deck and fooled with the throttle. He had always been edgy and strict about the engine controls. Evidently the engine had had problems before we ever got on board in St. Martin, and he didn't like what he heard. With São Miguel just a three-to-four-hour motor ride away, Dimitri turned off the engine and got out his tool set. And Yves and I put away our beers without finishing them.

For more than an hour the captain tinkered with the engine, cleaning and replacing the filters. We lay in our cabins waiting. There was little left to do. Our cabins were clean, our bags were packed. It was soon dark and I could see the lights blinking in Ponta Delgado. We were close enough to shore for the captain to call for help, if it was necessary, but we were not sinking and to be towed in would've been humiliating and expensive. Possibly, we would spend the night bobbing in the outer bay, lying in the direct path of freighters heading into the harbor.

In the end, the captain decided to start the engine and

continue toward Ponta Delgado at a slow speed. The engine sputtered but did not stall. The sea was dead calm. I went to the bow, peering into the moonless night. It was difficult to make out where we were. Between the lights on land, there were areas of such dense darkness it was hard to fathom what if anything was there. Had a bank of fog descended? Were deserted headlands and islands standing in our path? Only gradually, the unpopulated slope of a mountainside and the lit-up lap of the harbor beneath it took shape.

It was 1 a.m. on Thursday before we took the fenders out of the sail locker and entered the inner harbor, homing in on a red flashing light at the end of an unseen jetty. The town was utterly silent, not a car or person visible. A ghost town with yellow glowing streetlamps. It felt as if humanity had ceased to exist. I wondered if the predicted volcanic eruptions had occurred. If the pandemic had decimated the population. The heavy odor of cow manure wafted in the air, followed in a breeze by the scent of pasture and conifer trees.

We docked at a forbidding-looking concrete structure surrounded by tall, barbed-wire fencing—the customs area, but at night it looked more like a prison. There was no one there to help . . . or greet us. We were locked in for the night. It was not the arrival I had imagined. You could say it was its opposite.

I jumped off the boat to grab the lines and immediately fell over on the hard asphalt surface of the dock. I was rubber-legged after being at sea for so long. Like an astronaut on a foreign planet, I struggled to stand up and walk in a straight line.

Once we had tied up, I moved carefully toward the end of the dock. In the darkness I looked from the ocean we had just crossed to the lights of the town. It took a while to fathom how far we had come, to let it sink in that I was back on land and alive.

CHAPTER 28
Destinations

One morning a few days after our arrival in the Azores, I found myself in a valley of giant conifers and palm trees. The path, strewn with fallen white and red camellias, meandered past hot springs, blooming magnolias, and strands of white and blue lilies. Mourning doves and orange-beaked blackbirds sang from their hidden branch lairs. Mottled carp, their gold scales peeling white, rose to kiss the surface of the narrow canals. Sun and blue sky appeared through the dense undergrowth. I heard the distant low of cows waiting to be milked, the crow of a cock, the tinsel ring of a church bell. After being blinded by the briny sea for almost three weeks, it felt like I had landed in the Garden of Eden. Even better, it turned out I was not alone in paradise.

The morning after we arrived in Ponta Delgada, the captain woke me, tapping me on the shoulder.

"You have a surprise waiting for you outside," he said.

I was taken aback by the strong morning sunlight, by how late I had slept. I wondered what I had missed and wandered onto the deck still rubbing my eyes. The captain, Yves, and Nikos were grinning like children. There on the dock stood Stacy with a basket of croissants, brioche, toast, butter, and jam.

Stacy, whose busy life as an art specialist at Sotheby's had hardly slowed down over the decades, doesn't often get away from work. Her mother had recently died. Covid-19 was still threatening. It wasn't the best time for a vacation, and I had little expectation that she might come meet me in the Azores. When we talked on the phone late the night before, me at the end of the concrete wharf still reeling from the waves, she was at first vague about where I had reached her. Later in the conversation she finally confessed that she had secretly bought a ticket, flown to the Azores via Portugal the previous day, and waited for *Orion* to arrive. She was at that moment, she told me, about a half mile away, standing on her hotel balcony where she had a view of the harbor.

In the morning, my memory was blurred. I stepped onto the land, carefully, and went over to where Stacy was waiting, smiling a little self-consciously in front of the crew. It was good to touch her, feel her slim waist and her arms around me.

After gorging on the pastries, I hauled my wheeled duffel bag with my damp salty clothes stuffed inside along the sunny seaside esplanade and across the cobblestone streets to our hotel. We went up to our room and I took a long hot shower. We spent the next two and a half days in Ponta Delgada. At first I was unsteady getting around. The floors were slanted, the walls moved. During nineteen days at sea, I had lost over ten pounds. I was blissful, but also uneasy, still not quite certain if I was truly there on solid ground.

Yves also booked a room at the hotel for a night. The three of us returned to the harbor quay, sat in the sun and ate squid with riced sauteed potatoes, olives, and vegetable salad for lunch. For dinner I ordered marinated mackerel crudo and bacalao and I drank wine. I slept and woke up suddenly in the night, thinking I had to be back on deck.

In the end, Yves decided to stay on *Orion* for the next leg of the trip, a six-day sail to Spain. The following morning he left to get back on the boat. From our balcony I watched him walk briskly down the promenade with a bag of freshly washed laundry slung over his shoulder, like the sailors of yore, like Ishmael. It was hard to see my friend go. Without Yves's encouragement I never would've gotten on *Orion* or survived the trip. On board *Orion* he watched my back. But now he was part of a new crew Dimitri had taken on—they were six on board—and there were provisions to pack. In the afternoon I went to the docks to give the captain a gift and to say goodbye. I felt like a deserter. A part of me wanted to stay on the boat, to never leave it, to go on forever waking up and not knowing what to expect, what I would see, where I would be.

Dimitri was busy but kind, the way—to be fair—he usually

was. He gave me a quick bright smile and went back to work. I suspected I was not someone he would remember fondly. I'm sure at times I was an anxious pest who overreacted. I have wondered if the captain's rage was mostly in my mind, and I considered that he might have done everything right, at least those things a captain should or could be responsible for. How could I second-guess a man who spent his entire life at sea? Who had safely guided us through the storm?

I, too, like most sailors have been dismissive of weather forecasts—wind speed projections are particularly unreliable. But they are not useless. If they were, we would not have been one of the few, if not the only sailboat—we heard of—caught out there in that wild ocean. If the captain's intermittent outbursts of anger were justified, why did Yves, who *never* complains, crumble that morning "traumatized" by the scene on deck. Why were we surprised so often after dark in a gale reefing the sails night after night? I did not imagine the shit shows or the leaks in my cabin.

I stood on a promontory just out of town and watched *Orion* motor out of the harbor and turn east.

(As it turned out, their subsequent sail to the mainland was almost perfect until they were within sight of Gibraltar, where the boat was attacked by a pod of orcas. The rudder was so damaged by the orcas that they had to put in at Gibraltar and have the boat hauled out and repaired. Yves ended up on a train to Malaga, where he finally met up with Pamela.)

In Ponta Delgada, Stacy and I spent an afternoon going from store to store looking for paints. We needed some blue for the sea, some red for the lettering, and yellow for Henri's beak and gray for his feathers. When at last we found the paint and brushes, we went down to the rock jetty where generations of other transatlantic sailors have left their marks. Simple paintings on the dark boulders of sails and shells, dolphins and clouds, dates and names of boats. On a face of basalt, Stacy painted the bird, Henri, the blue sea, and a star.

EPILOGUE: SOMEWHERE

Where does the story begin?
How do you put an end to the past
and turn it into the present?
—Daniel Mendelsohn

Six months later, on a cloudy cold morning on the last day of October, I found myself crossing the Newport Bridge and seeing, in the distance on a hill overlooking the ocean, the church chapel of the school I had once attended as a teenager. It was there I first fell for the sea and sailing, there that I began to see the world as other boys and men see it, there that I was first tested. I may have succeeded then in a conventional sense by graduating and being accepted into Harvard, but there was a chasm inside me.

At school, lacking self-knowledge and confidence about who I was and where I belonged, I relied on my charm and savoir faire (not unlike my father) to get by. A classmate, a boy I hardly knew, who was a social outsider, the scion of a major manufacturer, wrote me a three-page letter from Greece (he was a budding classicist) after we graduated. He wrote that he had watched me from afar over the four years at boarding school and that he wanted to warn me that despite my accomplishments, I had been coasting on my charisma and one day, years from then, I would pay a heavy price. It took decades of experience, a master's in journalism, a book, piles of published articles, years of therapy, and this monumental—to me—voyage across the ocean to acknowledge the fission of self-doubt and paranoia churning inside. To cross the Atlantic was to face the ocean void within me. To survive the storm I had to stop conflating flaws for certain failure, challenges for disaster, a setback for doom. I had to slow the tick-tock of my troubled family history. My forebearers had crossed their sea of troubles, and now I had traversed my own.

A few months after my father died, my younger sister sent me a black-and-white photograph of my father I had never seen. In it he is a young man, about the same age I was when I graduated from St. George's. He is sitting on an adobe wall in his bathing suit, still wet from his swim, his mask on his head, the Mediterranean Sea behind him. It turned out my father loved the water and was, like I was for a time, on his school swim team. In the picture he is beaming and unburdened, an image of him, young and hopeful, that still astonishes me today.

Driving into Newport that morning, it was gratifying but also somehow embarrassing to be back, to be realizing things in my sixties many others in my class knew innately a long time ago.

In one boatyard I climbed a ladder to see a neglected boat, with puddles of dirty water in the cabin and a damaged rudder. The broker tried to convince me it was a good deal, but I was not swayed and moved on. I ended up at a marina in Portsmouth, Rhode Island, a few miles north of Newport. I walked down to the floating docks and there it was, still in the water at a slip, a junior version of *Orion*. A modest, thirty-one-foot sloop, made by the same French company, though half the name was now missing off the stern. Otherwise she was clean and in good shape. She had a furling main, like *Orion* too. She was twenty feet shorter, but the teak interior felt roomy with two sleeping cabins and lots of light. Three weeks later, on a blue, chilly day in late November, we took her out for a brief sea trial. The following week I bought her for the price of a pickup truck.

The boat is fourteen years old, so there were issues: a leak in the cabin roof; the blown pump in the head; an occasional jamming mainsail and fidgety self-pilot; fuses and broken latches to replace; a new radar, bimini, and solar panels to be installed.

I spent rainy, chilly spring weekends taking it step by step, talking over repairs with my young, stoned mechanics and solving the problems one at time. I was tempted to throw in the towel, to admit that I'd started this project too late in life, but my newfound patience, my love of the sea, its unpredictable moods, the calm rocking at night under the stars won out. By the end of April I was sailing the boat with a pro in twenty-knot winds to finesse my handling of the sails and rigging.

I had a calm, methodical coach. There was no yelling, no humiliating reprimands, no questioning of your manhood. Attitudes *are* changing. Today, more captains and sailing coaches have realized that positive encouragement and a careful attention to detail is more effective in training an inexperienced, perhaps tottering crew than shouting and intimidation.

For many sailors, heading out to sea is a deliberate decision to leave behind the ugly and destructive human behavior we witness all around us on land: the continual wars and atrocities; the torrent of vitriol and polemics that inundates us on the internet. Instead, some sail toward the empty horizon to find peace, a sense of union, of commonality with the sea, the stars, and each other. What is a boat at sea but a symbol of our collective soul in the face of an indifferent universe?

My boat, though, is not a metaphor. It's eleven thousand pounds of hull, keel, mast, sails, rudder, shrouds, winches, halyards, sheets, anchor, cabin, galley, head, hoses, batteries, wires, fuses, and engine. It's a self-contained complex world that demands my complete attention when I'm on board, and I hope one day to master it. I live for this understanding of the vessel, the wind, the waves, the sails, and the helm. It makes me feel complete.

By the first week of May, I had sailed solo on my boat, newly christened *Merci,* a handful of times and prepared her for the seventy-odd-mile crossing from Portsmouth, Rhode Island, to the East End of Long Island, where she would be moored a few miles from our house.

Yves, ever the loyal and encouraging friend, came up from New York by train to accompany me on the two-and-a-half-day trip. I was anxious to capture the last of a northeast blow, so after a quick lunch on board, we left in the afternoon for a short sail down Narragansett Bay to Newport, where we planned to spend the night. We passed under the Newport Bridge and furled the sails in the shadow of Fort Adams point. As the sun set, we drifted into a deserted Brenton Cove, the snug bay where Paul had once moored *Limbas* and taught me how to sail that summer so many decades before.

That evening as we drank our wine and looked at the church spires and docks of Newport Harbor, I reminisced a bit about the scrappy sailor town with run-down bars, tattoo parlors, and music shops that the town had once been. I talked about my parents and grandparents crossing the ocean, about their dreams. We talked about becoming Americans and how long it can take to feel like you belong. The next morning at dawn, the tangerine-tinted water whirled with the outgoing tide. Terns dipped to pick up spearing from the surface. We unfurled the mainsail of my boat and set forth for the open sea.

In the time since then, I've sailed on my own in high winds, against strong tides, and in dense fog. I almost wrecked the boat sailing with my old friend Paul when we lost steerage close to a lighthouse shoal in a squall. Together, though, we pulled through.

With each trip comes a sense of accomplishment. There is relief, too, as I drop anchor in a quiet bay after a windy day at the helm or I tie to my home mooring after being at sea for several days. But I'm always reluctant to leave the boat behind. As I pull away in the dinghy toward shore—and another reckoning with terrestrial life—I keep turning back to make sure *Merci* is still there, floating calmly in the waves waiting for my return.

ACKNOWLEDGMENTS

First, I wish to thank my steadfast friend Yves Duboin. Without his determination and enthusiasm, I never would have gotten on the boat, much less crossed an ocean. I'm also indebted to my schoolmate and old friend Paul Nevin, who taught me how to sail all those decades ago and whose assiduous notes on seafaring terms and ways greatly sharpened my manuscript.

This tale would not have made it into print without the encouragement and guidance of my editor, Bill Strachan, who helped mend my unruly sentences and shape the narrative of the two stories. Also, thanks to Pat Strachan for her complimentary asides and kind words.

Many errors were caught and perceptive suggestions made by my early readers: Elizabeth Williamson, Pamela Morgan, Michael Glazebrook, Fiona McCrae, Michael Hainey, and Pamela Farland. I so appreciate the time they took to underline, cross out, comment, or just urge me on.

Profound thanks also to David Michaelis, Peter Bodo, and Rebecca Chace for championing the book early on.

My appreciation goes out to my publisher, City Point Press and David Wilk, whose professionalism and experience were essential in getting the book out and on schedule with Simon and Schuster. Emily Wichland's rigorous fact-checking and copyediting were invaluable. Barbara Thomas—artist, fellow writer, and devoted friend—organized the first event in which I read from the book, then called *At Sea*, and was unfailingly helpful in spreading the word to the right people.

I owe so much to my family and my parents (now deceased). In particular, I would like to thank my sisters—Caroline, Guislaine, and Claudie—for reading and encouraging me to write about our past; my cousins overseas for sharing their photographs, memories, and stories; and Tonne and Wendy for cheering me on. Also, many thanks go to my dear friends Virginia, Daniel, Kristen, Jim, Bill, Annie, Elizabeth, and the others—you know who you are—for standing by me through the years!

To Stacy I owe it all, for the heart rock and her company while I wrote down the story.

Finally, though we had our differences, the outcome might have been far worse if it were not for the captain, who stayed at the helm throughout the storm and guided us to the other side.

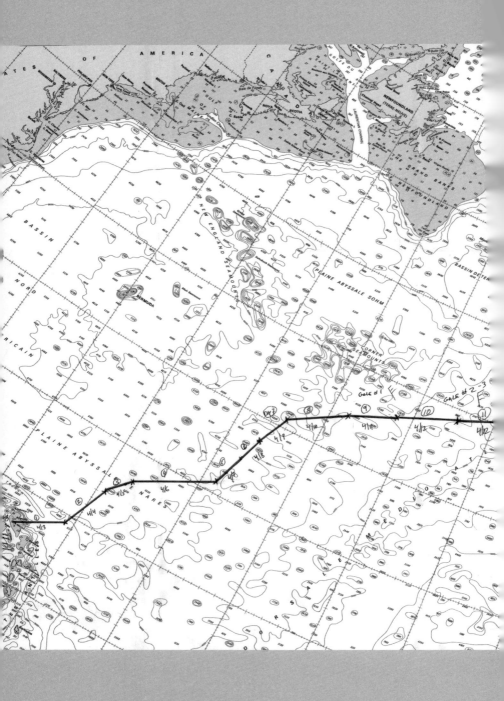